God, If You're Real, Let the Cow Be in the Pen When I Get Home

Ernest Dyess

Acts 22:15

God,
If You're Real,
Let the Cow
Be in the Pen
When I Get Home

Ernest L. Dyess

Scriptural references are taken from the *King James Version* of the Bible.

God, If You're Real, Let the Cow Be in the Pen When I Get Home by Ernest L. Dyess
ISBN 0-9641704-0-X
Library of Congress Catalog Card Pending
Copyright © 1994 by Ernest L. Dyess

Produced by:
Selah House
P.O. Box 257
South Plainfield, NJ 07080

To the Glory of God.

Contents

Preface

Is God real? I believe every person asks that question at some time in his or her life. Certainly no one can become a Christian until a decision is made that God is the Father and that eternal life can only be found through belief and acceptance of His Son, Jesus Christ.

But thank God that all the burden of reasoning about His reality does not rest upon our own shoulders. The Scriptures say, "I...will draw all men to me" (John 12:32); and "The grace of God that bringeth salvation hath appeared to all men" (Titus 2:11). So as we journey through life pondering the reality of God, the Holy Spirit is at work revealing himself to us. This book is about some of the ways God has revealed himself to me. I believe that He deals with each one of us separately and in different ways. But I am also thankful that His word states, "If you shall search for me with your whole heart, you shall find me,"

Sometimes we see God's reality in little things. For instance, being raised in rural Alabama I have always had a fear of finding a space when entering the flow of traffic on a busy interstate highway. "Lord, give me a vacant space with plenty of room." That prayer makes me know that the Lord is real and is interested in my welfare as He answers.

As I look back at God's revelations to me, I think of the first time, as a very young boy, when I asked God if He existed. I'll never forget that warm feeling of His presence while I stood in a freshly plowed field during the evening twilight when He assured me that the family milk cow would be in the pen when I got home. God became real that evening and I have known that He exists ever since.

Jesus came into my life while I was on a burning ship during a storm in the latter part of World War II. The Bible states that if I accepted Him, He would never leave me or forsake me. Over the years that promise has become reality. That's what this book is about—experiencing God's reality. If He lives within you and you know Him, you too have been experiencing His reality. If you have never made that decision for Jesus Christ, I hope He will reveal himself to you as you read these pages and you too will commit yourself to Him and begin experiencing His realness in your own life.

I also have a second hope as you read this book...that you too will catch a glimpse of how you can share Jesus with others.

Introduction

I began to think about writing this book after making a new commitment to the Lord in 1975. Following that commitment, I often rose earlier than usual for Bible study and prayer. I kept a prayer list which evolved into writing narratives of experiences where I had seen the reality of God. My thoughts of a book developed as I filled a note pad and continued to write about answered prayers and events the Lord revealed.

By nature, I am not an early riser. Getting up in the morning is my hardest chore of the day. But God seemed to give me clarity of mind when I was willing to get up. One by one, He allowed new things to happen which along with the old are recorded in this book.

A few months before I took early retirement on May 1, 1988, I purchased a computer and; with the help of Jim Bonner, a co-worker, I began to learn word processing. It's been three years since retirement and I'm still learning, and Jim is still helping.

Without Jim's help and encouragement, as well as some other people, I doubt that I would have finished the book. Perhaps that in itself is another way God revealed himself to me. He always sent someone to encourage me when I needed a boost.

In addition to Jim, another booster was Mrs. Viola Liddell, a gifted writer of two books and numerous articles for national publications. After reviewing a few of the chapters, Mrs. Viola gave me some good advice, plus encouragement to continue.

Keith Carpenter, the subject of chapter thirty-six, was another contributor and encourager. I met Keith while I was industrially employed and wrote a chapter about how God had revealed himself to us through a project we shared. After retirement, I called Keith and asked him to review the chapter. It was then that he also volunteered to do the illustrating and formatting for the manuscript. I believe God impressed him to contribute, just as He did the others, to help make the publication possible. Judy Bonner, Jim's wife, furnished her English expertise to help with the grammar. Alyce Yarbrough, Judy Powe, Will Philpot and Brother Eddie Davidson made their contributions as final proofreaders.

Last, but by no means least, is my family. My wife Rachel put up with me during my late nights of writing, made her suggestions and boosted my morale. Our children Steve and Denise, and their families, were always in touch and made their contributions. Ashley, who was in kindergarten when I wrote of her faith in chapter twelve, has become a computer whiz and helped with the final word processing.

When God calls us home, most of us want to leave something for our offspring. God didn't see fit to give me any grandsons, but He did give five gifted granddaughters. Both Ashley and her younger sister Amy have become young Christians. Denise's daughters, Rachel and her identical twin sisters Andrea and Erica, are still too young to understand salvation. As the girls grow older, I hope they can comprehend the legacy their grandfather leaves and they too will experience the reality of God by trusting in Jesus Christ as their personal Savior.

But the best efforts of people are put into proper perspective when we read Psalms 127:1, "Except the Lord build the house, they labor in vain that build it: except the Lord keep the city, the watchman waketh but in vain."

I, and I believe those who helped, give the Lord credit for "building" this book. It is to His glory that it is dedicated.

1

Let the Cow Be in the Pen

I felt sick. An empty feeling came into my stomach as I thought about our next meals without any milk. For a brief moment I considered braving the growing darkness and running across McDonald swamp into the wooded land beyond in search of Daisy, our family milk cow. But I couldn't do it. The scream of the panther was still too real in my mind for me to go near the swamp when darkness came.

It was the height of the Great Depression, the mid-thirties. My daddy had probably worked somewhere that day to supplement our meager farm income, sometimes for as little as fifty cents. We needed the milk. It, along with our potatoes, syrup, meal from our corn and other home grown produce, was our food.

I was about seven years old when it became my job to drive the cow from the woods to the pen each afternoon. There wasn't much grazing near our house, so the cow often went across the swamp where there was plenty of grass. That afternoon, as I often did, I had stopped to visit my cousin George who lived a quarter of a mile below us, before getting the cow. Whatever game we were playing must have been exciting because the dark shadows were settling over the swamp before I realized the day was far spent.

A trail by the swamp was the nearest way home; but I took a longer route across a freshly plowed field so I wouldn't be near the swamp. As the last rays of twilight faded into night, I prayed my first prayer of remembrance and asked God about His reality. "God, if you are real, let the cow be in the pen when I get home."

Both my parents came from families who were Primitive Baptist. My great-grandfather, Winfield Scott Dyess Jr., had given land for a church and cemetery. But the church didn't meet very often, so as a child I seldom went. However, I always took an interest when people talked about God. I had heard adults discuss prayer, and how God would answer when we had needs.

I was almost home when I prayed that prayer. I could see the dim outline of our farm house which Daddy had built, partly from pine logs. He had chosen a site on a gently sloping hillside overlooking the swamp on the back side of the Dyess place in Rosinton, Alabama. One of thirteen living heirs of Elijah Louis Dyess, he thought he might be able to keep his share on the corner of the property if the land was ever sold.

Daddy covered the house with cypress shingles he had riven from heart logs found in the local creeks. He made a rock chimney from native stones which became our family focal point during the winter months. Mama's churn, quilting frames hanging from the ceiling, and chairs ringed the area in front of the fireplace. But one special place was always mine, the wall next to the left side of the chimney where I would sit on the floor and read from the firelight of the fat pine knots we burned for heat. Two brothers and a sister joined the family, but I always claimed the space by the chimney. "Secretary Hawkins," a weekly feature in the Grit newspaper which I sold on Saturday, was my favorite reading material.

A hundred yards or so behind the house was a clear, bubbling spring which was our source of water. Mama washed our clothes there with an old fashioned rub board. When I was old enough, I kept the fire going around the wash pot and stirred the clothes with a stick. Then the panther moved into the swamp. He had his den somewhere near the spring and his terrifying scream came each night as darkness settled over the swamp. His cry, which sounded like the scream of a desperate woman, came once each night and it was usually near the spring.

Daddy decided something had to be done about the cat, so on one moonlit night he was waiting near the spring with his single-barrel shotgun loaded with buckshot. Mama and I waited in the house. Right on schedule there was the blood-curdling voice of the cat. In a few moments we heard the roar of the gun, followed quickly by daddy's arrival on the front porch. I think he chose to set a new hundred-yard track record rather than stay near the cat with an empty gun.

The cat's tracks were found the next day, but there was no sign to indicate he had been hit; however, we never heard or saw him again. Nonetheless, in my mind his presence was always there, especially when darkness came.

As I crossed the plowed field that late afternoon, I didn't want to go the last few yards to the house. Not only did I feel ashamed and depressed, but I also thought about the peach tree growing in the yard, and its long sprouts that sometimes became Mama's switches. The switch I could stand; the reminder I would get, probably more than once, that we had no milk because I played with George and didn't get the cow, would be the most difficult to bear. Yes, I had a need. If God was real, could He take care of it? I decided to ask Him.

That first prayer was as sincere as any I have ever prayed. At my young age, I wasn't thinking about the question of eternal life; I just wanted to know if God was able to fulfill a desperate need. I wanted that evening to be one of those very rare days when the cow came home without my driving her. Usually, if I didn't go get her, she would just lie down when night came and we wouldn't have milk the next day.

"God, if you are real, let the cow be in the pen when I get home," was my plea.

In that newly plowed field long ago, I first experienced the reality of God. He not only warmed my heart and assured me the cow would be in the pen, He also gave me a lasting memory of His presence and branded the scene in my mind as I have described it. I was over forty years old before I shared this experience with another soul. But I have never forgotten that moment when I knew there is a living God.

When I got to the house, Mama had already milked the cow and she never knew that I didn't bring Daisy home that night. The experience didn't make me a Christian. But the answered prayer completed my first step—a step that every person must make before he or she can become a Christian— believing in the reality of God and a resurrected Jesus.

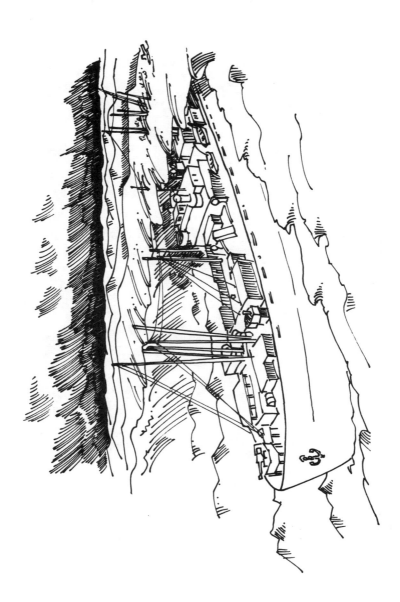

2

If This Ship Goes Under

When I was in the seventh grade, the Dyess place, which included our house, was sold through court action by its many heirs. Daddy thought he would be able to keep his share on the corner of the property where he had built our house, but it didn't work out.

We moved to Florida, stayed a year, then moved back to the Rosinton community. My high school years at Robertsdale were during the uncertain days of World War II. Friends and kin went away to serve, some never to return. Young men had to grow up fast because they knew their time of duty would come soon.

Everybody worked while we were waiting and growing up. One summer I worked as a lead hand in the fields with German prisoners of war who had been captured in North Africa. Two other summers I worked in the shipyards in Mobile helping build ocean tankers.

An experience in the shipyard showed me how

fragile life really is. Another young man and I were sent to string a wire for night lights along the railing of an overhead crane which ran on tracks. No one told us there was a bare copper wire next to the track that powered the crane. As we worked we stood on a metal pipe about thirty feet above the ground. The crane passed over and we ducked our heads. While we were crouched down, I saw a spark from the bare wire and I knew it was hot. There was lots of noise and my working partner, some twenty feet down the line, raised up and accidentally grabbed the wire before I could warn him. He couldn't let go of the wire. He caught his wrist with the other hand as he tried to free himself. Then he climbed over the top of the rail track, which was chest high, and fell to the ground in a pile of angle iron.

I can still see the agony of the pain on his face as he fought to free himself, and then his stillness on the ground below. I have also thought of how that could have been me.

I remember another time when I was coming out from under the hull of a ship. I stopped to remove something from my eye and in almost the same instant an iron wedge, dropped from high up the side of the ship, plunged into the ground at my feet at the very spot I would have been had I not stopped. These and other similar instances made me think about eternity while I was a young man. I had been to church enough to know that I could find salvation through trust in Jesus Christ, but I hadn't surrendered my heart to Him.

Early in 1945, a dozen of my schoolmates and I

decided to do our tour of duty in the Merchant Marines. My first assignment after sixteen weeks of training in St. Petersburg, Florida, was aboard the Liberty ship Harriet Monroe. The war ended while I was en route to board the ship in Mobile, Alabama. Its cargo was a load of coal destined for Naples, Italy. I remember the ship was already loaded to the low water line when I reported for my job as Second Cook and Baker.

I was glad the war was over, but it was still a time of mixed emotions for an eighteen-year-old youth as we passed under the guns of historic Fort Morgan which had guarded Mobile Bay for centuries. The familiar beach which I had often visited as a teenager while growing up a few miles away soon disappeared over the horizon. I felt alone for the first time since leaving home. My home town classmates were always there during maritime training. But now I was with forty crew members and two naval gunners who were still strangers as I left everything that had been familiar. I felt the pangs of homesickness and loneliness which can only be understood by someone who has had the same experience. Looking back, I think it was a time when God was dealing with me, drawing me to Him as He promises He will do to all people.

I could see bathers on the beaches as we passed around the Florida Keys and into the Atlantic Ocean. It was almost a month before I saw land again—and thirty-two days before we reached our destination. The sea remained unusually calm. I vividly remember a late afternoon after all the work was done in the galley. I took an orange and went on the deck to get the benefit of a cool breeze. I sat on the number three hatch cover and began eating the orange. As I cast the orange peels into the sea, my thoughts were of home and friends.

Before the trip was over, I would become good friends with Knobby Walsh, the Third Cook, who had been a football player at the University of Wisconsin. But that evening, as the sun cast its last golden rays across the calm sea, I felt outside the circle of human friendship. It was indeed the calm before the storm.

Knobby and I were cooking breakfast the next morning when the storm hit without warning. The first wave washed completely over the ship, sending a torrent of water into the galley through an open skylight on the second deck. All the food that was on the range flooded the galley deck, including a boiler of salt mackerel which some of the old seamen always wanted. We got the skylight closed and started the cleanup as the sea's heaving and churning continued to build in intensity. I had made several short training trips in fairly rough weather, but I had never been seasick like some fellow seamen. As we cleaned up the greasy fish, I found out the true meaning of motion sickness.

By the second day the storm was at the peak of its fury. One instant we would ride a great wave and break clear on top of the world for a few seconds, then suddenly drop into the trough between the next wave before being covered with water.

Then came our second problem. The coal in the number three hatch forward of the engine room caught fire from spontaneous combustion caused by the rough sea. The bulkhead wall joining the engine room became red hot and actually bulged out in many places. We were in danger of both an explosion and losing our power through a break in the wall. The raging sea made it impossible to open the hatch to control the fire on the already overloaded ship.

On the third day we were doing what we could to provide food for the crew when the ship's Bosun appeared in the galley. "Fellows, we just put out the S.O.S. emergency signal. We can't control the fire and we are taking on water, so be ready for anything. We are trying to make the Azores Islands, but we don't know how much longer we can stay afloat."

His next words triggered my decision for Christ. "It doesn't make any difference to me if it goes under or not," was the Bosun's comment as he prepared to leave the galley. I had grown to respect the Bosun in the short time I had known him. He had many years of experience and knew his job. But as I looked into his eyes, I saw not an indifference about death, but fear of its possibility.

I was afraid when the storm hit and more so after the fire broke out. Suddenly I realized I might soon go out into eternity without Jesus, forever separated from God. I knew that Christ had died for my sins and that He would save me if I committed my life to Him. For a long time I had planned to do that someday—but not yet. The expression in the Bosun's eyes made me realize that I might not have another day.

I quickly left the galley, found a place to be alone, and as best as I knew how, I asked the Lord to save me. I vividly remember that a part of my prayer was, "Lord, if this ship goes under, I want to be with You." At the time, I didn't know the story of the "thief on the cross" as recorded in Luke 23:33-43. The thief acknowledged that he was getting his due reward, but that Jesus had done nothing wrong, and then he asked to be remembered when Jesus got to heaven. By exercising his faith in Jesus, he was assured of his eternal destiny. Like the thief, I knew my lost condition and came to Jesus in a childlike way. I'm thankful that is all the Lord requires.

At the time, I felt that baptism was essential to salvation. I wanted to make sure that everything was right. I opened a hatch door on the opposite side of the direction of the waves, and holding on to a guard rail as the water washed across the deck, I baptized myself.

It wasn't long until we passed out of the storm, controlled the fire, and continued to our destination.

My current pastor at the Camden Baptist Church, Brother Eddie Davidson, recently preached a sermon using Psalm 107:23-30 for his text. The verses describe my experience:

> 23 They that go down to the sea in ships, that do business in great waters:
>
> 24 These see the works of the Lord, and his wonders in the deep.
>
> 25 For he commandeth, and raiseth the stormy wind, which lifteth up the waves thereof.

14

26 They mount up to the heaven, they go down again to the depths: their soul is melted because of trouble.

27 They reel to and fro, and stagger like a drunken man, and are at their wit's end.

28 Then they cry unto the Lord in their trouble, and he bringeth them out of their distresses.

29 He maketh the storm a calm, so that the waves thereof are still.

30 Then are they glad because they be quiet; so he bringeth them unto their desired haven.

I have heard of people being saved through many circumstances. My first pastor, Brother E. L. Roberts at the Pine Flat Baptist Church in Perry County, Alabama, said, "A person doesn't come to the Lord unless he or she feels a need. Usually they are going through some type of storm in their life."

I believe God made the real storm I have described just for me.

3

More Than I Brought

I stayed in the Merchant Marines almost two years. My last ship was a combination passenger-cargo vessel which was making a regular run from Mobile, to Puerto Rico, to New Orleans, then back to Mobile. It was an ideal assignment which gave me the opportunity to be home for a couple of days each month. I was saving some money with the goal of buying farm equipment so I could become a truck farmer in fertile Baldwin County. But when we got back to Mobile, my boss wanted me to get off the ship. He claimed I wasn't doing a good job. I found out later he wanted to give my job to a friend of his. I decided it might be best if I got off the ship.

Much has been written and said about Romans 8:28, "All things work together for good to them that love God, to them who are the called according to his purpose." I sure don't know all the theology about this, but I do believe God works good out of apparently bad things when we are trusting Him, and He is often working good when we don't even know it. It took me a while to realize it, but the frustration I experienced when I got off that ship led to God giving me one of the greatest blessings of my life.

I am sure God would have taken care of me and given me a good life as a truck farmer. The work would have been hard and the financial rewards uncertain, but I always liked to see things grow. When I was growing up, the neighbors often talked about the little gardens I planted and worked with a hoe in odd corners of the farm each year. My farming projects carried right on through high school as part of my vocational agriculture class. I had a great teacher and I often thought of how I would like to be a teacher like him. But I always dismissed the thought as being unrealistic. In the Depression years, college was a place that wealthy kids attended.

When I got home after leaving the ship, I was looking at a newspaper and read an article about the army seeking volunteers to replace overseas troops who had fought the war. Their pitch was that you could enlist for just eighteen months and still get the G. I. Bill to attend college. I saw this as a way to become an agriculture teacher. I had been very depressed when I left the ship, but I know now that God was opening the door to something more challenging and purposeful for my life.

Today, in my retirement years, He is letting me be that truck farmer I envisioned as a boy. Even this day, December 8, 1990, has been an especially joyous one. I completed putting up the posts for an additional acre to the muscadine vineyard. And many people came to purchase Christmas trees. I even shared the above story of my last voyage and the things that followed with a young couple who bought a tree. Isn't God good?

Another early experience of the reality of God happened at Fort Bragg, North Carolina, during basic training. On a Sunday afternoon we had our first free time and I decided to go to a movie. As I was walking down a hill from the barracks toward the area of the theater and PX, I began to hear church music over a loud speaker. I recognized that it was coming from a chapel in a little valley off to my left. The Holy Spirit spoke to my heart and urged me to go to the service rather than the movie.

Chaplain Honeycutt spoke that night. I don't remember what he said. I just knew that I needed to make a public profession of my commitment to Christ on the ship. I responded during the invitation and told the chaplain about my experience. After the service he asked me what church I wanted to join. I told him about the Rosinton Methodist Church where my friends attended. He said he would write them a letter and tell the church I had been baptized into the Methodist fellowship. That was my second baptism, which followed my own at sea. A third baptism came after I finished college and went to work in a Baptist community as the agriculture teacher in the local high school. I feel now that the baptizing let every one around me know that I had made a commitment to Jesus Christ. Salvation came when I trusted in Jesus, confessed my sins and asked to be with Him if the ship went under.

I attended church regularly while in the army and college. I don't believe I could have been happy if I had not been in church and a consistent reader of the Bible.

In 1951 I received my B.S. Degree in Agricultural Education from Auburn University. At almost the same time God opened the agriculture teacher's position at Suttle High School in Perry County and put me in the right place to get the job. Sixteen years later the community gave me a going away party when I resigned after accepting a new job with MacMillan Bloedel, a forest products company who was building a new paper mill, sawmill and plywood complex at Pine Hill, Alabama. A very supportive co-worker, Jean McVay, made the comment that I was taking more with me than I had brought. She was right, because other than myself, I had brought nothing.

First, there was Rachel, a very pretty young lady who caught my eye the first time I saw her. But there was a problem: She was going with another guy. I dated some other girls, but the more I saw of Rachel, the more she rang my bell. I remember one night being outside the teacher's apartment where I lived. It was dark, with only a little moonlight. I got serious with God. "Lord, if she is the one for me, open the door," I prayed. God heard that prayer and a few weeks later we were married.

I was also taking two fine children, Steve and Denise. I was taking a thousand fond memories: of young men I'd watch develop into manhood; of adults who were more than friends; of special times of ball games and hunting and fishing expeditions.

I was leaving with the title to 288 acres of land that I had been able to buy on a school teacher's salary. I am convinced that the land, and all my other physical possessions, came as gifts from God through an important scriptural principle I learned from the Christian witness of my first principal, R. H. Hall and his wife. Rachel and I hadn't been married long and were struggling to meet our financial obligations. We were discussing our difficulties with the Halls when Mr. Hall said, "We used to have trouble with our expenses too, until we started tithing."

Mrs. Hall added, "The first check we make out each month is for the Lord's work; then we live on what's left."

Rachel and I discussed tithing. We didn't see how we could do it but decided to try. A couple of times I tried to postpone the tithe. Each time the Lord collected it. I recall once in particular after He had given us the farm. I had bought an old tractor and Steve and I were using it to pull trees that had grown up in the abandoned fields we were clearing. We would dig around the trees on one side, cut the roots with an axe, tie a cable to the tree, and pull it down with the tractor. We had barely started when one of the rear wheels almost came off after a cuff broke which held the wheel to the axle. The cost for a new one was the amount of the tithe which I had postponed. The Lord expects me to keep my commitment, but what He has done for me cannot be measured by human standards. There should have been no way for us to buy the land on a school teacher's salary, but God worked it out. I never made a whole lot of money teaching school; however, there were other things that replaced the money. For example, my children were never sick and it didn't cost much to live in the rural community. God has been real to me through all my finances. We cannot out-give God!

Yes, I took a lot more away than I brought when I left Suttle. But all that I took was made available because of the reality of God.

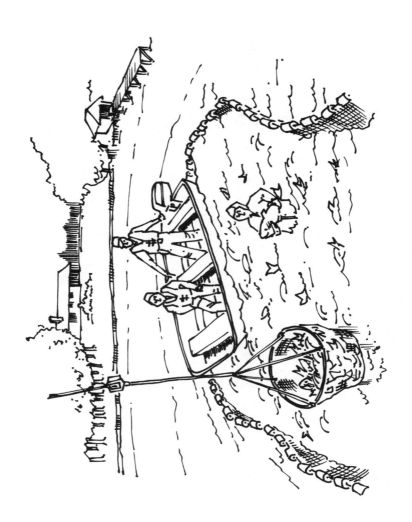

4

Go Into the Catfish Business

Trust in the Lord with all thine heart; and lean not unto thine own understanding. In all thy ways acknowledge him, and he shall direct thy paths (Proverbs 3:5-6).

I doubt that anyone else would have heard the voice if they had been with me that Sunday afternoon when I asked God for direction for what seemed to be a wasted investment. But the message, "Go into the catfish business," sounded from the trees and was as audible as a two-way conversation— or so it seemed to me.

For months I had been trying to put something together for the building of a fourteen-acre lake on the seventy-five acres of land I had located in Wilcox County after taking the new job with MacMillan Bloedel. I had made a down payment with the equity from the house we had sold in Perry County with the idea of subdividing the land around the proposed lake and keeping about twenty acres for our house site. I planned to charge enough on each sale to pay for building the lake, which would be owned by each family. Then I would invest the remainder of our equity into building a house.

I had the commitment for one tract from a fellow employee before I made the down payment and mortgage for the land. But his wife saw a movie in which a family's two children drowned in a lake. They had two children, and she decided she didn't want to live by a lake for fear they might also drown. "I told you I would buy the land and I will, but we won't build there," said my co-worker.

"No, I'll find someone else if you don't plan to use the land," I told him.

Although several people were moving into the area as the mill was being staffed, I hadn't found any other buyers. Land was not easy to find, but the undeveloped site was hard to visualize. Sometimes a man might be interested, but the wife would throw cold water on the deal when she saw the place. "You aren't moving me out into those woods," would be a typical reply.

So it looked like I had bitten off more than I could chew in buying a tract of land which I couldn't pay for and building a house at the same time. I was a very discouraged man when I drove from our rented house to the property one Sunday afternoon. I walked out into the swamp where the lake was to be built, sat down on a log, and prayed as humbly as I knew how, "Lord, what am I going to do?"

The Lord's answer, "Go into the catfish business," was one of the highlights of my Christian experience. I knew He had spoken, although I knew little about raising catfish and had not even considered that as a possibility. My original plan was to grow bass and blue gills in the lake for the enjoyment of all the participating landowners.

The next week I talked to Les Johnson, president of the Camden National Bank, and told him about my new plan. "Sure you can get the money. We will also give you a construction loan to build your house; then you can get other long-term financing," said Mr. Johnson.

Years later when Les and I were discussing the changed plan, he commented, "You got to keep the whole place and you probably avoided a lot of problems that would have come with several people owning the lake."

We built the lake and became a local pioneer in catfish farming in 1972. We usually grow a crop of catfish every year and God has blessed us to make a profit which helped pay for the place and buy other things during the eighteen years we've had the land. I know I am not worthy for the Lord to have given us this place and the other good things He has bestowed, but I have tried to acknowledge His goodness to others and use the lake as a testimony to His reality.

For example, early this summer I had to make an addition on the feed house so we could buy feed in larger amounts for hauling convenience. I had two inmates from the Work Release Center helping with the work and one of them asked how I happened to get into the catfish business. It was the perfect opening I had been waiting for to tell them about Jesus. "Why don't we take a break and have a cup of cold water and I'll tell you," I said. Before we finished I was able to tell them of God's voice to go into the fish business and how they too could become Christians and surrender their lives to Christ. I shared with the men how God blessed us to make enough money from the fish and other income to eventually pay for the lake construction and land. "God wants to give us good things in this life and eternal life in our lives to come," I said.

I presented the plan of salvation that morning and as we ate sandwiches at lunch, I gave each man a tract. Rachel told the men about a sermon Billy Graham had preached on television the night before. Billy had said that our lives were like tape recorders in which God records every thing we have ever done. "God is the only person who can erase the tape and forget our past. When we accept Jesus, He does that and remembers our sin no more. We start life over with a new tape," Rachel quoted from Rev. Graham's sermon as the men listened attentively.

We don't always know the results of such a witness, but I do know that His Word will not come back void until it accomplishes His purpose. I don't think anyone ever forgets a witness about our Savior.

While we were still without a preacher, I spoke at our church's Wednesday night prayer service and related another time when God had allowed me to use the pond work to tell someone about the

Lord. After the service, one of the ladies, Crescentia Wilder, who had been in my Sunday School class years before, reminded me that I had shared many events about the pond with the class.

If we are sensitive to the Lord's leadership, we will hear and see Him in all our activities.

5

I Heard the Music of Heaven

The new job I took with MacMillan Bloedel in 1967 as Training Coordinator was demanding but exciting. After purchasing the seventy-five acres of land, I built the fish pond and started construction on our house. I was burning the candle at both ends. I doubt if I would have admitted this at the time, but a normal day consisted of eight or more hours on the job, then coming to the house site and working until about 10:00 P.M. I would go home and eat the evening meal Rachel had prepared after also working on the house during the day. The family spent all day at the house site on Saturday. We reserved Sunday for church and rest.

When we started the house, we had decided we would not be involved in midweek activities at the church until we finished. However, when the time came for the summer revival, we discussed leaving off the night work. With some reservations, we decided we should attend. I don't remember what the revival was about, but a conversation I had with

Jim Andress, a young man who had recently come to work for MacMillan Bloedel, reaffirmed my faith about God's rewards when we put Him first.

After the service, Jim and I were talking outside the church. In the course of our conversation, I mentioned our work on the house and Jim responded, "I want to build a house some day. Could I come and help you in the evenings after work just for the experience? You don't have to pay me anything, I just want to get the experience."

Jim was faithful to come almost every evening. His wife, Kay, also came with him many times on Saturday. We became lifelong friends. I know God sent Jim and Kay at a time when we needed them most. We had already been working a long time on the house and it seemed we were making little progress. Rachel and I were both discouraged. Jim and Kay gave the mental and physical boost we needed to keep going. I don't think we would have made it if we hadn't stopped and attended the revival and received God's blessing.

Even with the extra help, it was July of the next year before the house was finally completed. We had moved in a few weeks earlier and then completed the den with old barn siding. Our son Steve was home from college for the summer and was working at MacMillan Bloedel. Throughout the two-and-a-half years of house building we had not taken much time for recreation such as hunting and fishing. Steve and I had a goal to finish the house before the Fourth of July holidays so we could go to Florida on a three-day fishing trip. Our last carpentry job was putting up the trim work around the carport. Rachel and Denise were the painters. They would put the finishing touches to the trim once we finished, and then the long project would be over.

When we arrived home from the mill on July 1, 1974, we still had about four hours of daylight, plenty of time to finish the job. However, I noticed that my energy level seemed low and it became more and more difficult to climb the ladder. Finally the last piece of trim was cut and nailed in place.

Steve quickly dressed and rushed off to town to see Diane. They were to be married in six weeks and there were many things to discuss. I walked down the hill to feed the catfish. The last rays of sunset were casting long shadows from the shoreline trees across the fourteen-acre lake as I loaded the pond boat and carried the feed out into the deep water. The fish were still churning the water eating the floating feed as I pushed myself back up the hill in the almost full darkness.

I settled into a reclining chair and began to reflect on the milestones of my life and think about the future. Now that the house was finished, I'd be able to get back to my hunting and fishing. I felt pretty good about my earthly security as I half watched a dull baseball game and thought about the fishing trip.

Sometime during the game I dozed, waking just as it was over. Still half asleep, I started for our bedroom, but a new sensation startled me into full wakefulness as I crawled into bed. My back had a tremendous ache. My arms began to hurt right down to my small and ring fingers. It almost felt as if someone had stuck a knife into my back at the base of my shoulder blades.

I got out of bed, then tried to lie down again, but this gave no relief. So I got up quickly and leaned upon a chest in front of a mirror. My face was without color and perspiration covered my forehead. I could both see and feel my life draining away as I accepted what I knew all along was happening to me. Only a few weeks before, I had read the symptoms of a heart attack printed in the November, 1973, issue of Reader's Digest, and I knew I was having one.

While I leaned on the chest, even though it was only a short time, a lot of thoughts ran through my mind. Knowing that people often died of heart attacks, I suddenly realized this might happen to me. "It's too late to change anything about my life," I thought. There were a lot of things I still wanted to do. A great emptiness came over me as I realized the incompleteness of my life. My earthly security, that only a few minutes ago had felt so good, suddenly lost all meaning.

About this time Rachel came into the bedroom. She recognized my condition immediately and began to try to call the doctor. I knew I needed to get to the car, knowing that I was growing weaker and weaker. I pulled on my trousers and started down the hall. As I passed Steve's bedroom, I saw through the open door, which he usually kept closed, that he had just come in—at least an hour earlier than usual. I remember telling him, "Come go with me, I'm sick," while I continued to move as rapidly as possible toward the carport. As I went out the back door, I knew I could go no farther and fell on the hood of the car for support.

Steve grabbed me and got me into the car just before I passed out. He took off for our small county hospital in Camden while Rachel was continuing her effort to locate the doctor. Steve later said I fell over on the seat next to him, my eyes bulged out and he thought I was dead. I was out almost two minutes, judging from where we were when I revived.

I guess I did die for a while that night, because I didn't want to come back. My first sensation was that I had left my body. It seemed as though I was in the car but not in myself. I remember seeing the dirt road we were traveling, the trees beside the road, turns in the road and then the beautiful music came. I don't know much about music, but I had never heard sounds like that before. It seemed to be pouring out all about me. It was so soothing and joyful that I didn't want to wake up. I remembered exactly where the car was when I first heard the music, in spite of the fact I was lying prone on the seat.

Dr. Sumpter Blackmon was waiting at the hospital. He gave me emergency treatment, including an electrocardiogram, and then ordered an ambulance and accompanied me to a Selma hospital thirty-five miles away.

During the long ride, I thought about praying that God would spare my life. I decided it was too late to pray in that way, so I just resigned myself to His care through Dr. Blackmon and the two well-trained volunteer ambulance drivers. I remembered my salvation experience at sea. I had the assurance of a home with the Lord, but I also had the feeling of not being ready to meet Him.

When we got near Selma the drivers blew the siren a lot. The sound seemed to penetrate right through me and I wished they would not use it. By the time we arrived at the hospital, my veins had collapsed and the nurse had difficulty inserting the glucose needle. Again, I almost had the feeling of leaving my body while the nurse was working with the needle. There were two pictures in the intensive care room, and they seemed to be spinning like a top, but the instant the emergency treatment was given through my veins, the pictures stabilized and my critical period was over.

The quick actions of my family, a concerned doctor and a well- trained staff, all under the direction of God, had allowed me to recover from what otherwise would have been a fatal attack. Within two months I was back at work, and other than a couple of times when I overexerted myself, I had no more serious physical trouble.

I don't believe the Lord let me hear the music and then come back because I was someone special. As I recognize all my weaknesses and failures, I think the opposite is true. I do believe He let me have the experience so I can share it. I think He wants all His people to know that heaven is a beautiful place with a wonderful choir we can enjoy when He calls us home.

Over the years I have shared the experience many, many times. Other people who have had near-death experiences have verified hearing that same heavenly choir. I especially recall Mrs. Lucy Hausey of the Catawba Springs Baptist Church near Brewton, Alabama. Rachel and I were part of a lay team helping with a revival in their church and we were staying in the Hausey's home. I had shared my experience and I noticed a smile on Mrs. Hausey's face as I tried to assure them of the pleasant journey we can expect when we leave this earth—provided we know Jesus as our Savior.

I thought she doubted the story until she said, "My father, a very saintly man, died a few years ago and the last time I saw him alive. he talked of beautiful music. 'Hear how pretty it is. But I forgot , you can't hear it,' he said as he came and went during his last hours."

I am convinced that it is just as Jesus said to the thief on the cross after he acknowledged his sins and asked to be remembered by Christ when He got to His kingdom, "Today shalt thou be with me in paradise" (Luke 23:43). It will only be an instant before we will be with Christ after death. We need not fear the hour when we know Him. It will be a joyful time which will stretch into all eternity.

6

Something Missing

It was the first week in April, 1975, when the Camden Baptist Church and the Camden Methodist Church hosted a lay team from Wednesday night through Sunday. The Lay-Led Revival had been set up through Bob Lambert, a former member of the Camden Baptist Church, who had moved to Athens, Tennessee and had become part of the team.

Although I was an active member of the Baptist Church and was on the board of deacons, I approached the revival with mixed emotions. I was looking forward to hearing the speakers each night, but I didn't want to be a part of the daily visitations which they were asking the church members to help with. I was a busy man, so I just made plans to be busy each day. I was the chairman of an annual spring turkey hunt to raise money for a private school, so that (along with my regular job) would take most of my time. After all, I didn't know these people, and they might embarrass me if I took them to visit some of my friends.

But two things happened during the week that changed my life. First, as I heard their testimonies and learned that many of them had taken vacation time from their jobs and driven long distances to be in Camden, I began to examine my own commitment. Secondly, the first speaker on Wednesday night, Charles Bair from Adariville, Kentucky, shared how God had spoken to him saying, "If I should call you home, who will you bring with you?" I asked myself that same question and came up lacking.

Charles shared that he was the primary owner of a bank which had become the center of his life, although he was regularly in church and had taught a Sunday School Class for many years. "When God posed His question, I tried to claim a couple of fellows who had been in my class, but finally decided that they had become Christians because of someone else's teaching and witness. When I admitted this to God, He said I was right, that I had been busy—but not about His business," related Charles.

Charles said that God then impressed on him the idea of selling the bank. He thought that he would get around this by agreeing to do so if God would send a buyer. To his surprise, a man walked into the bank wanting to buy it. Charles said that they agreed on a price only to have the man say he didn't have the money. Again Charles thought he had an out when he said 'no money, no deal.' But the man went to a lending institution in Nashville and they agreed to loan him the money.

Charles said, "I thought I had done God a big favor, and I told Him I was now His man." Charles expectantly waited for the Lord's call to service. He admitted, "The Lord had to teach me humbleness and for six months I heard nothing."

Finally God put him with a lay team. He shared an event that happened on his first trip during a visit to a bitter truck driver who said he wanted no part of God, even if it meant hell. "As best as I knew how, I shared with him the love of Christ; but his heart had been made bitter because of an unbelieving father," said Charles.

"When I was a young boy, I went to a tent revival near our house," explained the driver. "I came home and told my daddy that I was going back the next night and get saved. He told me not to go back down there, that what they were saying was not so. He even threatened to whip me if I went, so I haven't had anything to do with God since."

Charles said he and the local church member were about to go when the Lord impressed on him to ask the man about his young boy, who was playing on the floor. "You say you don't care about going to hell, but what about your son? Do you want him to go there, too? " asked Charles.

"No, I don't want my son to go there," quickly responded the man.

"But your son is probably going to be like you, just as you are like your father. Unless you change your mind and accept Jesus as your Savior, he may never do so either," said Charles. According to Charles' testimony, God touched that man's heart because he loved his son. Tears began to run down his cheeks and he knelt on the kitchen floor and asked Christ to come into his life.

"He was a big man and I thought he would crush my ribs as he hugged me and thanked me many times for telling him about Jesus. As we left that trailer, I was walking on air. I knew now there would be someone to go with me when Jesus called me home," concluded Bair.

I continued to avoid the daytime visitation during the Camden revival, but I looked forward to the testimonies of the two people Brother Fred Pinkard, the lay team leader, would call upon to share each night. I especially remember Dr. Ernest Forster from Dayton, Tennessee. He could be in Camden only one night, but he had driven the 350 miles to share his testimony. He told of being saved as a young boy in Pennsylvania, attending the University of Tennessee, serving in the military and then beginning his medical practice in Dayton.

"I completely forgot about God during college and my military years," said the doctor. "But late one night a nurse came to me at the hospital in Dayton and said that a ten-year-old girl I was scheduled to operate on in the morning was hysterical. It seemed someone had asked her if she would go to hell if she died during the operation. I thought of calling a preacher, but it was late, so I decided to talk to her. When I finally got her calmed down, she asked me, "Doctor, if I die, will I go to hell?"

I could think of only one thing to tell her. "No, honey, if you believe in Jesus, everything will be all right." That seemed to satisfy her and she was soon asleep. "I left that room with a great feeling, and for the first time in a long time, I again realized the reality of God. I began to look for the opportunity to tell people about Jesus," said the doctor.

Even though it's been over sixteen years since I heard the doctor's testimony, it made a lasting impression upon me in relation to my commitment to witness. The same doctor told another very vivid experience which God used to touch me as well. "One morning the police brought a young man to the hospital who had gone berserk because of taking drugs. He had a big gash on his head when they picked him up on the street. I tried to talk to him but his mind was irrational, so all I could do was sew him up. I had to let them take him to the city's padded cell, because we had no place for him in the hospital. I worked all day and forgot the man until I got to an intersection on my way home that evening. I literally couldn't turn my car in the direction of home and immediately thought of the man in the cell. In spite of the fact that I was tired, I drove to the jail and asked about the young man.

"His head had cleared and they let me in the cell with him. He was dirty and smelly from his life on the street, but I put my arm around him and told him I loved him and that Jesus loved him. I found that he came from a good family, but the drugs had led to his present condition. Jesus touched that young man as I shared His love, and he invited Christ into his heart. I wasn't tired anymore as I left the jail and drove home. But that wasn't the end of the story. About two weeks later, a man came into my office and said, 'Doctor, you don't know me, but I just wanted you to know that I was outside that cell when you came to the jail and shared Jesus with that young man. And I have found Him, too.' So many times we may be witnessing and not even know it," commented Dr. Forster.

Approximately fifty lay people, from many vocations of life, came to Camden to work with the two churches. Some had little education but they were filled with the spirit of God's love. When the invitation was given following the Sunday morning service, I knew something was missing in my Christian life. "If you have a problem, come to the altar, pray about it and God will take it," said the morning speaker, Fred Pinkard.

That morning I was one of the deacons seated on a front row seat, scheduled to help usher and take up the collection. Pride may have kept me from visitation, but God had done His work in me through the lay speakers and I responded. As I knelt at the altar, I said a simple prayer, "Lord, something is missing in my life. Show me what it is." And then I went back to my seat. That prayer changed my life.

God let me see myself as I really was as He began to show me what was missing. I saw myself far more as a "give-me Christian" than as someone who reached out to others. I thought there was only a certain amount I needed to do to satisfy God, such as attending the scheduled church services. If I attended the services on Sunday, and usually Wednesday, that should be enough, I felt.

So don't ask me to do something on Saturday, my heart murmured. That's my day—I've already paid my dues. I had received a couple of promotions on my job, but I wanted more—so my job was more important than the Lord. Since I had been raised a poor boy—the farm was also too important.

God showed me many things that night, but the greatest thing He showed me was my unconfessed sins, sins that I had swept under the rug and thought I could keep hidden. That was surely the most miserable week of my whole life, and before it was over, I knew I had to do something about my condition. I talked to my pastor, Tommy Davis, and asked that he give an invitation for recommitment following the morning service.

When I went forward, I told Brother Tommy that I was giving my job, farm and family back to the Lord. I recognized that these were His all the while, but I had been claiming them as personal property. I also implied that I wanted to make a new start and be what the Lord wanted me to be.

Brother Tommy did something I hadn't counted on, but I am glad he did because it sealed my commitment. "Why don't you tell the church what you just told me," he said. I did that and also urged anyone else in the congregation who might need to make a similar commitment to do so. No one did, but Tommy asked Rachel and me to stand in front and invited the church fellowship to speak to us after the service. As the membership came, I felt a great peace as God lifted all the burdens off my shoulders, some of which I had carried for years.

Two other things happened that day for which I shall forever be thankful. First, God gave me the eternal assurance of my salvation. Most of the time since I had accepted Christ as my Savior when I was a young man, I had that assurance. I don't remember not having peace about my eternal destiny since the heart attack, but there were times before when I wasn't sure. I recall speaking to Rachel's grandfather a few months after his wife died. Brother Willie Morgan had served the Lord faithfully as a country preacher for about fifty years in Perry County, Alabama. I asked him how he was feeling, "Not too well. I am ready to go be with my wife now," he said just like he was ready to walk into the next room and she would be there.

I said to myself, "How can he be so sure?" God had taken away my assurance because of my emphasis on things of the world. In John 10:10 Christ said, "I am come that (you) they might have life. and that they might have it more abundantly." I now believe that the abundant life is the assurance of where we will spend eternity.

That same day God gave me the desire and boldness to share His good news with others. Having been a Sunday School teacher, I should have already been at this plateau, but I was not. I remember a man in one of my classes raising this question about salvation, "How do you know when you are saved?" It was one thing to go over the Scripture and teach some highlights of the commentary, but quite another to explain the plan of salvation to a man who is searching for the truth. I don't remember exactly what I told him, but it wasn't the answer he needed. Praise the Lord that he did find what he was trying to understand later and became a Christian through someone else's help.

Although I didn't make a single visit with the lay team in Camden, two months later Rachel and I found ourselves in Vernon, Florida, as new members of the same lay team. During the second visit I made, I saw a lady get saved in her home through the power of the Holy Spirit and the witness of an experienced lay team member. This happened after a neighbor had said there was no need to go to that house. I came back home with a new vision for soul winning and a few weeks later had the experience of praying with an inmate in jail to receive Christ. After that experience, I could echo Charles Bair's testimony, "Now there will be someone to go with me."

7

Our Ways Are Not the Lord's Ways

For my thoughts are not your thoughts, neither are your ways my ways, saith the Lord (Isa. 55:8).

The year was 1979 or 1980. Rachel and I had been out of town for the weekend and we were returning to the community on Sunday afternoon. It was spring time and my garden was beginning to grow—new pecan grafts were beginning to bud. I couldn't wait to get home to take my leisurely walk about the place to see how things had grown.

As we passed a house where a church family lived who were assigned to me as part of our family ministry plan, I had a strong feeling that I should stop and visit. The urge was so great that I am sure the Holy Spirit was telling me to stop for a special reason.

In spite of a commitment I had made to try to follow Christ, I found reasons not to that afternoon. I accused the devil of trying to disturb me. "I have been gone all weekend and need to get home to see about things. Lord, I'll go Tuesday during my regular visitation night," were my comments to the Lord. But my real reason was that I didn't want to give up the remainder of the afternoon before church time, even though the urging of the Spirit continued until I was almost home.

Tuesday night I called the family in anticipation of a visit, but they were not home. I failed to make contact for several weeks before I finally was able to visit, a visit that was at best only social and without fruit.

I have passed the house many times since that day and each time I am reminded of my failure to be obedient to the leadership of the Holy Spirit. I have asked the Lord's forgiveness. I guess He has granted it because His word says in First John 1:9 that He will, but I have had a hard time forgiving myself.

I went back to see the family at other times. I even confessed my failure to them. When I asked if they knew of any reason I should had visited that afternoon, they said they knew of none. But I know that God had a reason. Maybe there was a visitor there waiting for someone to share Jesus. Maybe it was the right time to share something with a family member before they passed into eternity. I am sure that I won't know until I bow before the Lord in heaven. Why do I feel so strongly that God had a special assignment for me that Sunday afternoon? First, I believe that every Christian knows when he fails God. Secondly, an event that happened several months later was God's clear revelation to me that He does prod our hearts through the urging of the Holy Spirit.

One afternoon when I was coming home from work and thinking about my failure to make the visit, I was passing another house and had the same feeling that I should visit. It too was a strong urging, although not as intense as before. I had planned to do some things at home that afternoon, but this time I didn't dwell on them. My only thought was, "Lord, you will have to lead me as to what I should say because I hardly know this man."

The man's name was Guy Kelly, the former County Superintendent of Education before his retirement. As I drove up his circular driveway, I found him standing on the lawn just as if he was waiting for my arrival.

As we talked, I identified myself as a member of the Camden Baptist Church. "Yes, your church prayed for my son when he had a brain tumor," said Mr. Kelly.

Mr. Kelly related that he had reached the depth of discouragement for his son on a Sunday afternoon while he was in a hospital in Pensacola, Florida. "I decided to leave the hospital room and walk around the grounds for a while. As I walked down the hallway, I passed a man who turned around and stopped me. 'Mister, I am just an old, worn-out Baptist Preacher, but if you are having a problem, maybe I can help.' I told him about my son and he said, 'Why don't we pray for your son?'

"When we got to his room, he put his hand on my son's head and began to pray. I never heard anyone pray like he did and almost immediately my son started to get better. Today he's back on his job and doing well."

I continue to be amazed at how God gives us leads, or openers, when He wants us to be His witness. Mr. Kelly's next statement opened the door for my witness to him. "Why do you suppose that preacher stopped me and came back that day?" he asked.

"Mr. Kelly, that was the Lord's doings. Just as it was the Lord who impressed me to stop as I drove by your house this afternoon. May I ask you about your salvation? Do you know that if you died today, you would be with the Lord?"

Mr. Kelly dropped his head and said, "No, I do not know."

" Would you like to know?"

"I sure would," was his quick reply.

I took out my Christian Life New Testament and went through the plan of salvation, then gave him an invitation to ask Jesus to forgive his sins and come into his life. He quickly accepted and there on his front lawn bowed his head and asked Jesus to save him.

Mr. Kelly related that he had been in church much of his life, but he had never asked Jesus to save him. All I know is that he was a different man when I left that afternoon. He was a man full of joy, and full of thanks, which he verbalized several times. "Thanks for stopping, thanks for stopping," were his parting words over and over again.

I left rejoicing that I had been there when God saved Mr. Kelly. Mr. Kelly died very suddenly of a heart attack about a month later. I was sorry to hear about his sudden death, but I rejoiced that I knew he knew Jesus.

I'll see him in heaven some day. I can only hope that God took care of my other assignment in another way.

These two events have taught me that God's ways are not man's ways, neither is His timing the same as ours. If we are His disciples, we just need to be sensitive to His leadership to witness to those He puts in front of us. This means we are sensitive as we go about our daily routine, in addition to our formal visitation times.

The urging of the Holy Spirit to be His witness, and then seeing Him work in our witness, is another way God reveals himself to me.

8

God's Multiplication Table

I will...pour you out a blessing, that there shall not be room enough to receive it (Mal. 3:10).

Warren Huggins, a bi-vocational preacher and an accountant who works with me at MacMillan Bloedel, is one of my best friends. We often meet for a few minutes at lunch time and share our problems, needs and blessings. Warren recently related the following chain of events:

"My church gave me fifty dollars for my birthday and I decided I wanted to buy a sliding glass back window for my pickup truck. When we make trips with the camper shell on the back, we can't talk to the children unless we stop, so I thought it would be nice to have a sliding glass window which we could open for our conversations. I went to our local Western Auto store and they had one for $34.50—but it wouldn't fit my truck. During a lunch hour. I went to the Camden store but had the same results. I said, 'Lord, you must not want me to have the window.'

"A few days later I was attending our Association meeting and saw a pastor friend, Don Twilly. His wife had been ill and I knew his finances were strained. God impressed me to give Don the fifty dollars. 'But Lord, the church gave the gift to me,' I said. Nevertheless, I gave Don the fifty dollars, saying it wasn't much but I hoped he could use it.

"The next week I was in the Bruce Cogle Ford dealership, which is going out of business, and their entire stock was being sold. On the floor was a back glass for a pickup. The price was five dollars. It was no longer in a box, so I didn't know if it would fit or not, but for that price I couldn't lose. When I got it home, I had it installed in a few minutes, a perfect fit."

God's blessings for the fifty dollars were multiplied fivefold. First, to the church for recognizing Warren for his faithful service. Then to Warren as he gave to a needy pastor. Then to Brother Don Twilly as he received from God who has promised to take care of all his needs. And on to Warren again as God renewed His covenant of goodness to those who are obedient to His leadership.

And last, but not least, finally to me as I hear about the reality of God in other people's lives.

9

Will I Die Next?

I first met Bealie Harrison in 1980 while serving on a committee to select one State and three Regional winners for the Helene Mosley Memorial Forestry Award. Rev. Harrison's farm had been selected as one of the finalists for the recognition.

We had started our work three days earlier in north Alabama, crisscrossing back and forth across the state . The Harrison farm in Clarke County was the last stop for our tired committee. But the bubbling enthusiasm of Rev. Bealie and his deep love of the land soon revived us as he explained his forest management plan on each unique location. I could sense that here was a man who loved living and working and being a good steward of God's resources. When all the criteria were considered, the committee selected him the Southern Regional State winner.

I wasn't surprised to learn three years later that Rev. Harrison had been selected by the American Tree Farmers Association as one of the five best

Tree Farmers in America for 1983. For his home forestry improvement efforts, leadership and enthusiasm in promoting forestry among non-industrial land owners, he was selected from more than 27,000 tree farmers in thirteen southern states and named "Southern Tree Farmer of the Year."

The Clarke County Forestry Committee made plans to have their annual forestry tour on the Harrison farm and to recognize the family for their accomplishments. I was one of the guests for the tour.

It was a delightful day. A caravan of farm tractors pulled hay wagons loaded with guests across a clear creek and along the winding roads that led through stands of young and old pine and hardwood trees which had been made more productive through a lot of hard work by the Harrison family.

"Trees are like a crop—you have to keep the weed trees out and space them properly for best results. Sometimes if you don't have a stand of desirable trees, you have to take them all out and start over," said Mr. Bealie as he talked to the group about his forestry work at each location. I don't believe anyone who owned some trees failed to catch a vision of what they too could do on their farm, after hearing the enthusiasm of Rev. Harrison.

But the best vision which Rev. Harrison portrayed was yet to come. When the tour was over, we gathered on the Harrison lawn under some large shade trees where a platform had been erected to recognize the Harrisons for being selected the "Southern Region Tree Farmer of the Year."

After the awards were presented and the speeches concluded, Rev. Bealie said, "Anytime I get a large crowd like this, I want to talk a long time. But I won't do that. I do want to say that we should all remember that only God can make a tree. He made these trees and everything else in this world for man's use, and He wants us to be good stewards of His gifts. More importantly, He made man and He wants us to find meaning for our lives, and He wants us to find a meaningful relationship with Him through Jesus Christ our Lord. If you fail to find that, you have missed it all. If I can ever help any of you, please let me know."

I left the tour that day knowing that I wanted to go back for additional material so I could feature the Harrisons in the *Perpetual Harvest*, a publication I edited for MacMillan Bloedel. Through various agencies I was able to get a lot of material about the forestry improvements performed by the Harrison family on their tree farm. I wrote a draft of the article for the *Perpetual Harvest*, and made a date with Rev. Harrison to make pictures and review the article.

It was a beautiful "Indian summer," fall day when I arrived at the Harrison home. He ushered me into the family den where a fire felt good after the morning chill. He and his wife reviewed the article, then Mr. Bealie and I headed to the woods for pictures to support the story. Not far from the house we passed by a cemetery. "Is that a family cemetery?" I asked.

"I suppose you could call it that. Many of my family are buried there. In fact, I have two children out there," he said as we drove into the woods. I inquired how they had died.

"The first to die was our youngest child who developed a stomach blockage. We first carried her to local doctors who thought the child had a virus. When it grew worse, we carried her to Selma and they discovered the problem, but gangrene had already set in by the time they operated, and the child died. A short time later, my five-year-old daughter was diagnosed as having leukemia and was soon dead. Within a few months I had lost two of my children, and I couldn't understand why," said Rev. Harrison.

By this time we had reached the swinging cable bridge which the Harrisons had built to cross Satilpa Creek during high water. As I got out my camera equipment, Rev. Harrison continued to tell me about his children. "I had just surrendered to preach and I told the Lord I couldn't understand why this was happening to me. I even questioned Him about some people I knew who didn't walk with Him who seemed to be doing better than I. About this time my heart almost broke when my eleven-year-old daughter crawled into my lap one night and asked me if she was going to die next, since she had just lost her younger sisters."

"What did you tell her, Mr. Bealie?" I asked.

"I told her I didn't know, but since she believed in Jesus it would be all right. If she died, she would just go live with Him. That seemed to satisfy her and she never mentioned dying again. But it was not so easy with me until I read in the first chapter of Job, verse 21. "...The Lord gave, and the Lord hath taken away; blessed be the name of the Lord." This verse jumped out to me. Suddenly I realized it was God who had given me the children, and for whatever reason, He had taken them away. Just as Job, I was to bless the name of the Lord.

I don't know why God took my children, but I do know that in all my years in the ministry, I have been better able to comfort families who have lost loved ones because of my own experience," he concluded.

A year or so after writing the article, I attended a Southern Forest Institute meeting in Atlanta where Brother Harrison had been invited to talk about his experience in the National "Tree Farm" contest. He gave an interesting talk about the Tree Farm program, but interwoven within the talk was a testimony of his relationship to the Lord. Business men from all over the South had to examine their own faith and relationship with the Lord after hearing Brother Bealie's talk.

Whether we are preachers or lay people, I believe this is what God would have us do—be His witness as we go. God has been more real to me through the life of Rev. Bealie Harrison.

10

God Still Does Miracles

Is God still in the miracle business as He was when Jesus walked the earth? Does He still perform miracles—such as healing the blind, or cleansing the leper, or raising the dead, or healing the lame?

Miracles were the subject of our discussion at the Camden Baptist Church's Wednesday night service sometimes during the mid-1970's. I recall making a statement that I felt Jesus did miracles during His life on earth to let people know He was the Son of God. He didn't heal everyone, but He healed many so that His glory might be recognized. I said He still does miracles in which He will be glorified by letting people know that He still lives today, just as He did when He walked the earth as flesh and blood. Little did I realize that the Lord would let me see Him do both a spiritual and a physical miracle the next day.

I got up early the next morning to drive to Opelika, Alabama. MacMillan Bloedel had a sawmill there, and I was assisting in a training program for its employees. By dawn, I had driven about eighty miles and was approaching the eastern bypass in Montgomery when I noticed a man walking up the southern ramp. I felt led to pick him up. He told me he had gotten a ride to Montgomery early in the night, but no one had picked him up as he walked the southern bypass. "I had just walked on the Interstate when you stopped," he said.

He said his name was Ray Murphy. He had been to Louisiana to visit some friends to help forget a broken marriage and divorce he had recently gone through. "My wife ran off with another man and the court gave me custody of our two children. I couldn't take care of them and work too, so I had to place them in a foster home," Ray confided.

"It sounds like you have a lot of problems, but I know someone who can take care of them," I said as we drove on the almost deserted Interstate. "Do you believe in Jesus?"

"When I was about fifteen years old, a friend of mine dared me to join the church with him during a revival in the community where I was raised. I never was one to not take a dare, so I went forward with him and was later baptized. But I have never been back to church since. I only did it because he dared me," said Ray.

"Ray, that was almost blasphemous," I said. "But Christ died for all our sins, and if you believe in Him and ask forgiveness for your sins, He will save you. Let me tell you what He has done for me." I shared with Ray the first time God became real to me when I prayed about the milk cow. I shared my salvation experience at sea. I was telling him about the heart attack and hearing the heavenly music when he interrupted me.

"I almost died once," he said. "When my little girl was ten years old, I took her to a "go-cart" race track in Columbus, Georgia. I had bought her a go-cart and she was good with it. They were having a race for ten-year-old boys, but the man in charge wouldn't let her enter because she was a girl. We got into an argument, and he hit me over the head with a baseball bat. He broke my jaw in two places. The doctor at the hospital told my wife I would not live through the night. I lived, but I have never been able to hear out of my left ear since."

I looked at the tired man beside me, maybe thirty-five years old, and my heart went out to him. "Ray, do you still love your wife after all that's happened?" I asked.

I wasn't surprised when he said, "Yes, I still love her. I would take her back if she would get herself straightened out."

"Ray, the Lord is able to put lives and marriages back together when we become Christians and trust Him. I can't say what He will do or or will not do. But He will do what is best for us when we trust Him, because He loves us. Would you like for me to share with you how you can become a Christian so you can let Christ give you the life He wants you to have?" I asked.

"Yes, I want to know," said Ray.

I reached in my back pocket for my Christian Life New Testament, "Ray, I want you to read what the Bible says about becoming a Christian; then you won't have to take my word for it."

The light traffic enabled me to help Ray find each Scripture. We started with John 3:16. Ray didn't read very well, but with my help he was able to get through each verse. "For God so loved the world, that he gave his only begotten Son, that whosoever believeth in him should not perish, but have everlasting life." I told Ray that God loved him. That he could insert his name in place of the word "world." The verse would then read, "For God so loved Ray, that he gave his only begotten Son (Jesus), that if Ray believed in him he would not perish (go to hell), but would have everlasting life."

We talked about sin. I explained to Ray that we were all sinners and that sin was doing things that displeased God, such as breaking the Ten Commandments. We found Romans 3:23 which Ray read aloud, "For all have sinned, and come short of the glory of God." Ray acknowledged that he was a sinner, that he had broken God's laws many times. We went on to Romans 6:23: "For the wages of sin is death; but the gift of God is eternal life through Jesus Christ our Lord."

I asked Ray what a gift was. "I guess it is something somebody gives to a person." I agreed with Ray and explained that a true gift had no strings attached.

Then I was led to give Ray this illustration: "Ray, suppose I wanted to give you this Bible as a gift. Whose Bible would it become?"

"I guess it would be mine," he said.

"That's right, it would be yours. You did nothing to earn it. All you did was be willing to receive it. However, let's suppose we had a flat tire and I said, 'Ray, I gave you my Bible, so I think you should fix the tire.' If that happened, then the Bible would no longer be free. You see Ray, salvation is a gift. It has been paid for by Jesus through His death on the cross when He redeemed us from our sins. It was a terrible price He had to pay; but He did it because He loves us, just as we talked about earlier."

I talked to Ray about the grace or goodness of God as written in the second chapter of Ephesians and how we are saved through faith and not of ourselves. Then I explained that salvation is the gift of God, not of works, lest any man should boast of being his own savior.

I asked Ray to turn to the tenth chapter of Romans so he could see how to receive the gift of salvation. It took a while for him to find the passage, but I waited so he could see the words himself. I asked him to read verses 9 and 10. Ray read slowly, but with a little help was able to finish the verses. "That if thou shalt confess with thy mouth the Lord Jesus, and shalt believe in thine heart that God hath raised him from the dead, thou shalt be saved. For with the heart man believeth unto righteousness; and with the mouth confession is made unto salvation" (Rom. 10:9-10).

"Ray, what do these verses mean to you?" I asked.

"I guess they mean you just have to believe and ask to be saved," he answered.

"That's right. Let me tell you about Revelation 3:20 which says, 'Behold, I stand at the door, and knock: if any man hear my voice, and open the door, I will come in to him, and will sup with him, and he with me.' What that means, Ray, is that if any man will open the door to his heart and ask Jesus to come in, He will. We can do that at any time and any place when we are ready to repent of our sins and ask for salvation. You can do that right now. Would you like to ask Jesus to save you?" I invited.

Without hesitation, Ray said, "Yes, I want to be saved."

Ray asked me to lead him in his prayer. I assured him that the words would have to come from his heart to Jesus. Ray prayed, "Lord Jesus, I know I am a sinner, I thank you for dying for my sins, I ask you now to forgive my sins and come into my heart and save me. Thank you Lord for saving me."

"Where will you go now when you die?" I asked Ray when the prayer was finished.

"I am going to heaven," he quickly responded.

"How do you know?" was my next question.

"We just read it in the Bible," was his ready answer. I knew then that Ray's faith would take him to heaven.

We were silent for a moment, only a few miles from the Opelika exit, then I noticed Ray begin to rub his head with both hands. He broke the silence with, "My head feels funny."

"The Holy Spirit comes to live within us when we accept Jesus. He promises that He will never leave us or forsake us. Some people say they have felt the presence of the Holy Spirit as He comes to dwell with us. Maybe that's what you feel," I said.

Again Ray was silent; then he began to pull on the lobe of his left ear. Suddenly he spoke out in an excited voice, "I can hear out of my ear again. I don't have to turn my head to hear what you are saying."

"Praise God. He has done a miracle in healing your ear. He didn't heal everyone when He walked the earth; but He did heal many so people would know who He was. He healed you for a purpose. He'll want you to go back to that church and tell them what happened; and He will want you to tell others about your healing miracle," I said.

"I'm going to do that," promised Ray as we turned off an Opelika exit. Ray had already told me that he was going to the home of a Lee County Deputy Sheriff who was a friend of his. He would help him get to his home somewhere in the county. As Ray directed me, I noticed it was the same route to the mill that I traveled. We kept going until he pointed out a house about three blocks from the mill site. I didn't have to go one inch out of my way to see God do a miracle.

Ray and I had prayer, then he got out and I have never seen or heard from him again. I don't know if he went back to the church, or if he ever told anyone about God's healing miracle. I do know that I will see Ray in heaven, because I saw the greatest of all miracles—the miracle of salvation. I also know that when it is in His will, God is still in the miracle business.

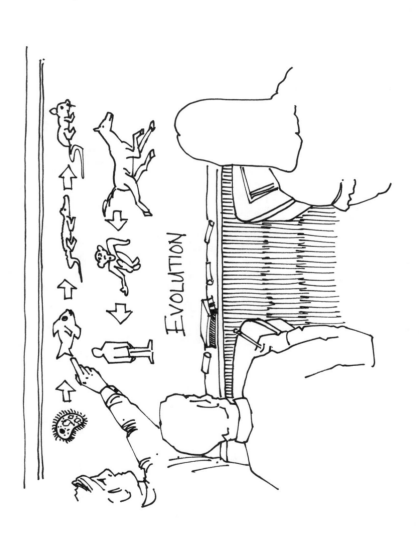

EVOLUTION

11

No One Spoke for Jesus, Including Me

After serving in the Merchant Marines and then the Army for a year and a half, I started my college work at Livingston University in the fall of 1948. I transferred to Auburn University, then known as Alabama Polytechnic Institute, in the summer of 1949. It was during that summer that I received my first real confrontation and I learned that some people just didn't believe there is a God.

I attended church regularly after becoming a Christian, both during my service in the military and in college. I can remember witnessing to my roommate, "You need to get right with the Lord, eternity is a long time to spend without Jesus," was one of my comments. But I was silent, as were the other fifty or so students, in a zoology class at Auburn when the young professor said he didn't believe there was a God.

"We're here through evolution. Man evolved from lower animal life through millions of years, and not from any divine creation. There's an order

73

to the universe, but I don't believe that a God created man or the earth. The books of the Bible which Moses wrote were written just to control the people" And so went some of his comments to the class as we studied the various animal kingdoms.

I don't know what the thoughts of the other students were as the professor spoke of his unbelief. I am sure there were other Christians in the group; but like me, they remained silent. I had always respected authority and Satan began to work on me through this. I began to doubt my own salvation as I thought, "The professor is a smart man. Maybe he's right."

Through this time of self-doubt, I kept reading my Bible. Then one day God used a simple verse to restore my faith as I read Jesus' conversation with Nicodemus about salvation (in the third chapter of John). "The wind bloweth where it listeth, and thou hearest the sound thereof, but canst not tell whence it cometh, and whither it goeth: so is every one that is born of the Spirit" (John 3:8). The verse jumped out at me.

The Lord seemed to say, "You don't know where the wind comes from but you do know it is there. Salvation is by faith and trust in Jesus." As the peace of the assurance of my salvation returned again, I thought, "If I knew all the answers, I'd be like God."

I liked the professor in spite of his unbelief. However my liking him didn't help with my class work. I struggled with the long names of the animal kingdoms and their sub-species. The final test was about a week away when I went to him with the question about the possibility of passing the course. "Let's see what your average is on the first four tests," was his comment as he took out his grade book. My average was 57. It took 70 to make a "D". "If I was a betting man, I'd bet you won't pass," was his final comment as he closed the grade book.

By this time I had an idea about the type of questions the professor would ask on the final, which would cover the entire course. I went to my room and spent several hours making a set of index cards from my notes. I lived with those cards until the test and made the second highest score in the class which brought my average to 76.5. It took 77 to get a "C," but I was still proud of the "D." Little did I realize that this test would be the subject of another conversation more than twenty-five years later.

Rachel and I were in a Lay Revival in Murfreesboro, Tennessee. about 1976 when Fred Pinkard, the revival coordinator, shared about another student at a well-known university who had an experience similar to mine. It happened at the height of an often-quoted popular phrase, "God is dead," which followed the publication of a book by that title. A visiting professor came to the university to do a series of lectures. The student, a young man studying for the ministry, was attending one of the meetings when the professor said, "Jesus Christ's blood has no more power than the water running out of a spigot."

God spoke to the young student and told him what to do. He was a poor boy and he knew if he obeyed God, he would probably be thrown out of school. So he said, "Lord, I'll pray about it."

The Lord said, "That's not what I told you to do."

The young man rose and began to sing, "There is a fountain filled with blood, drawn from Immanuel's veins, and sinners plunged beneath that flood, lose all their guilty stains."

Fred said the place became very quiet as the young man began to sing. He had already resolved that he would sing until they threw him out. He finished the first verse and started the second when another student rose and joined him. In a moment there was another and another and then the whole room was standing and singing with him. The professor stared at the students for a while, then took up his notes, left the room and never returned to finish the remaining scheduled lectures. Fred concluded the story saying, "Always remember that you plus God make a majority in any situation."

Many times since my college days I have wished that I had been more bold and spoken out about my faith in the zoology class. That night in Tennessee I made God a promise: "Lord, if the professor is still alive and you will make him available, I'll go talk to him about your reality."

My son Steve, then a student at Auburn, was home the next week end. I shared what had happened with him and asked that he check the phone books to see if the professor was still in the area.

"He's still teaching and he's the head of a major department," said Steve on his next trip home.

I asked the Lord to make him available to me. Almost immediately I was invited to go to Auburn and present a part on the program for a Teacher's

Conservation Workshop. I left early on the appointed day so I would have time to see the professor before my spot on the program. "He's not teaching this summer, but he often comes to his office; however, he is not here today," were the words of the receptionist in his departmental building. My feathers dropped as I silently prayed, "Lord, if you want me to see him, let him be here when I finish the program."

"He just came in," was the greeting from the receptionist when I returned to the departmental building that afternoon. Amazingly, the professor remembered me after all those years. I reminded him of the test and we had a big laugh about his motivation tactic.

"Professor, the real reason I am here is to talk about some of the things that have happened to me since I finished school." He was quiet as I briefly summarized my Christian testimony, highlighting the heart attack when I felt my spirit leave my body and heard the beautiful music of heaven.

"I don't have any doubt that there is a God, and a heaven and life after we die," I said. "In the zoology class, you said you didn't believe that was so. Has any thing happened to make you change your mind since?" I asked.

He got out of his chair without replying and walked to a shelf and took out a book. As he opened the cover, he said, "We have seventeen different nationalities in this department. About a year ago, one of the professors wanted to start a Bible study for them. I felt led to buy reference books which my church was using for a study course at the time. Let me show you what's in the book." The first title in the contents page was, "How God Created the Earth." He read several others which I don't remember, but one dealt with Moses leading the people out of Egypt, and another with how Christ died for man's sins.

The professor then shared two experiences of how God had revealed himself to him. Once was during a tornado when several houses around him had been destroyed and his was left undamaged. But it was a Baptist preacher, on a Pacific Island where he was doing some work, who had led him to the Lord. The preacher had a young son who was flying his kite when it became entangled in a high-voltage power line supported by a metal-constructed post assembly. The boy climbed to the top to get his kite. The professor said he came in direct contact with the electrical power and then fell to the ground far below. "Miraculously, he was not injured. His leather jacket had a hole burned through the front from the high voltage line. He got up, ran to the house and told his mother that the Lord had something special for him to do. That something special was to make religious movies, which he is doing today," shared the professor.

We shared other events of how God had been real in our lives that afternoon. One statement I remember most was, "I know I said some things to students that were not so, and it has bothered me," he confided as I was about to leave.

My reply was, "Well don't let it worry you, because it made me examine my faith and I came out stronger."

I learned later that the professor retired and left the area. I haven't seen him since that afternoon when we had prayer together before parting. To me, the whole chain of events is another confirmation of the reality of God; and also of His promise of grace that brings salvation to all men, as stated in Titus 2:11.

Every person, even the strongest atheist, gets a visit from the Lord. We only have to open the door when He knocks. I'm glad the professor opened the door and humbled himself before the Lord and asked for salvation. As I left the professor's office that day, I no longer felt so bad about not speaking out for Jesus in the class years before.

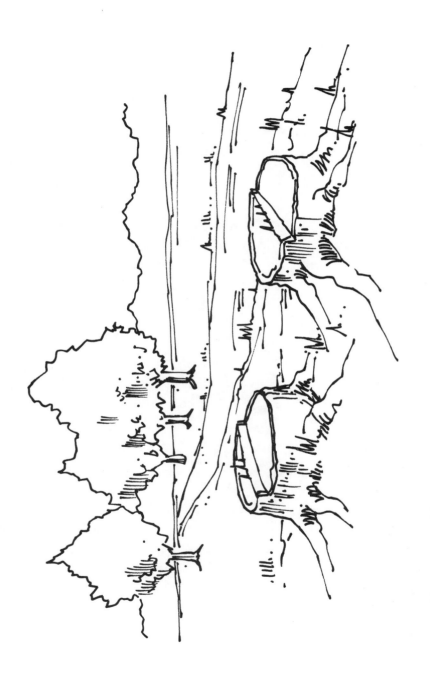

12

Cedar Stumps and Restitution

The two cedar stumps seemed to hold my attention as I walked along the roadway bordering my eastern property line in Perry County. My thoughts went back almost two years when I had last seen the stumps after cutting the trees and splitting them into fence posts. Each detail that led to the cutting of the trees flashed into my mind.

I remembered my plans to plant pastures and build fences on the farm land we had purchased in Wilcox County. I had just bought a new chain saw and was on my way to the Heighburger community with permission to cut some cedar for fence posts off land the Company had purchased. The land was not far from our camp house in Suttle where I planned to spent the night and then cut the posts on Saturday. I'd never split cedar before, so it was going to be a new experience.

I arrived at the camp house well before dark on Friday afternoon. I remembered some cedar was growing along an old roadway near my property line. The idea came that I could try out my saw and also see how cedar would split into posts. I drove to the backside of the place where the cedars stood, only to see that they were not on my side of the property line. I wanted to cut the trees pretty badly, so I began to rationalize, "The Company has that land under a long-term lease, so the timber will be cut before long. They don't use cedar, so it will be pushed up and burnt with the slash. I might as well make some use of it," was my rationale. So I proceeded to fell the trees. They split easily and I soon had fifteen posts worked out. The next day I cut a truck load of posts at Heighburger.

Every event of the week end became a clear picture as I looked at the two stumps. A lot had happened in the two years since I had cut the trees. First, the heart attack, then the Lay Revival and a new commitment to Christ. As I looked at the stumps, God's Spirit seem to say that I needed to get things right with the owners of the property.

Again I tried to rationalize. "Lord, you know that the trees would have never brought the estate any money." Again I reviewed with the Lord that the trees would have been burned in the windrows after the timber was cut.

"But they were not your trees," was the reply of the still, small voice.

The administrator of the estate had a reputation of being a firm businessman who always collected everything that was owed. I didn't want to go see him and confess what I had done. Too, I thought about my own reputation in the community where I lived for almost twenty years. I certainly didn't want it known that I had taken something that was not mine.

"Lord, I just can't do it," was my thought as I agonized about how my reputation would be destroyed.

But there was no peace, and I knew I must do what God wanted. When I finally said, "Lord, if that's what you want, I'll do it," the calmness returned which can only be given by God.

I went to the administrator's office, told him what I had done, and asked to make it right.

"What do you want to do?" was his question to me.

"I'll either bring the posts to you, or pay you whatever you think is right," I answered.

"We don't need the posts, but I can tell you want to get this thing off your conscience, so you tell me what the trees were worth," was his reply.

We agreed on a price and I paid him. I don't know if he told anybody the events or not. No one in the community ever mentioned it to me if he did. But once I had made things right, it didn't seem to matter. The Holy Spirit has led me to share the story on several speaking occasions. I think that's what following Jesus is all about. It's admitting our failures as well as talking about our victories. Jesus died for our sins, and through His shed blood we are made whole again. First John 1:9 states, "If we confess our sins, he is faithful and just to forgive us our sins, and to cleanse us from all unrighteousness."

The awareness of God's reality comes in many ways. It can be through our obedience to correct wrongs after the prodding of the Holy Spirit. As I have grown older and made new commitments to try to be what the Lord wants, He has revealed other fleshly failures which need correcting. Usually the confessions have been hard to make. But once made, God again restores the peace that passes all understanding and becomes more real in the next adventure of life.

13

When Things Break Down

Sometimes when I have work goals set, nothing seems to fall in place. Such was the case a couple of weeks ago when I was trying to get the pond bush hogged while it was dry, the pond sludge hauled to the pecan orchard, sand filled in the bottom of the holding pond and the shallow part of the pond deepened with the blade. Each job required the use of the tractor.

Unfortunately, this was the same period of time when the hydraulic system on the tractor decided to develop a leak. The leak wasn't too bad, so I just decided to keep adding oil rather than stop and lose time getting it fixed. Then I got the tractor stuck in the holding pond and had to call a wrecker to get out.

The leak got worse, so I called Tommy Richards, who sometimes worked on the tractor. He couldn't come, but said he would get me a small part and he thought I could fix it. Two days later, after driving to Catherine some twenty miles away, I had the parts and Tommy's instructions. I hurried home optimistic that my limited mechanical ability would soon get me started again. I had to disassemble several parts of the tractor to get the line off before I could attempt to make the repair. I felt good about the job as I reassembled the parts, but when I cranked the engine the leak was worse than before.

A shade of my confidence was missing as I very carefully repeated the job and cranked the engine. No leak. I decided I must be a pretty good mechanic after all, in spite of the five hours spent on the job.

There were still a few hours of daylight left, plenty of time to make a good showing, as I had determined to do each day since retiring. With a surge of the throttle I put the tractor in reverse and backed out of the shed ready to get back to the bush hogging. Suddenly the tractor was a gusher of oil. The ferrule which was supposed to clamp around the line when the jam nut was tightened had slipped completely off the line and the hydraulic oil was spraying like a water spout.

Discouraged, I cleaned up the oil and disassembled the line again. "Lord, if you want me to go get a new line from the tractor dealer, that's what I'll do tomorrow, even if it is seventy-five miles away," I prayed as I made one last effort to fix the line.

I consider myself a slow spiritual learner. I have recognized, however, that God sometimes wants to put someone in our path to share the way of salvation or to give a word of encouragement. I had a feeling that my last effort wasn't going to work either—that it would be more productive to go get a new line.

Before leaving the next morning, I made some notes of parts I would need on the back of a tract called "Four Spiritual Laws." It started to rain for the first time in weeks as I walked into the equipment dealer's building. In a very friendly way the salesman got the needed parts, told me what I had done wrong when I was trying to fix the leak and ordered me a new steering rod, which had been damaged when I got stuck.

I didn't think that my real purpose for the trip was to get the parts. When the last part was ordered, God showed me the perfect opener to share Jesus, "I don't need this booklet any more, but it has some good information in it. It tells you how you can get to know Jesus Christ if you never had a personal experience with Him," I said.

I shared some things Christ had done in my life. I told of feeling yesterday afternoon that I needed to come and get the parts. While we were talking the phone rang several times, but in spite of some reluctance to listen, he came back each time as I shared how Christ was real to me. When I finished, I encouraged him to read the tract and left knowing that I had been obedient to the leadership of the Holy Spirit.

On the way home, I stopped in Camden and told a young mechanic, Mike Vick, about my experience with the line. "I've got a minute, let me come out and help you get it on," he said. He not only helped me get the line on again, but we also adjusted the brakes and, more importantly, had a long discussion about the reality of God.

A few days later the new steering rod arrived, and I decided to call the tractor dealer and ask him how it should be installed. He told me what I needed to know. "Did you read that booklet I gave you?" I asked when we finished discussing the tractor.

"I sure did, and I took it home and let my wife read it," he responded.

I assured him that getting things right with the Lord was the most important business we'll ever do on this earth. "If we miss Jesus, we miss it all," I stated. We closed our conservation without him ever telling me if he had made things right with Christ. I pray that he has. But one thing I have learned—I can't save anyone. Only Christ can do that. Our job is to be the witness.

I am also learning that when things break down, or just plain don't turn out like I want, to look for a blessing that Jesus wants to share.

14

Glenda's Deer

January 10, 1984

It was a cold, clear morning as I left our camp house in Perry County at the crack of dawn for an early morning deer hunt. It was a perfect day to be in the great outdoors and enjoy God's gift of nature.

I crossed the dam which held the water for the four-acre lake and continued up the hillside along the woods road that circled the lake, moving very slowly in hope of seeing a white-tail deer. As I began to crest the hill, I came to a clear area under some young pine trees overlooking the lake. I leaned my 30.06 rifle against a pine tree and knelt on the ground, giving thanks to God for allowing me to come to our special place again, a blessing that had become more meaningful after the heart attack.

For me, this is a special place, a place I had set aside as my altar to communicate with God after He miraculously gave me the land on a school teacher's meager salary. It was my place to go when I came back to Perry County, a place to remind me each time I passed of God's reality and His goodness to me.

When I finished my prayer, I continued my slow pace along the old roadway with the rifle in a ready position. A hundred yards from the altar, my mind went back two years to this very spot where I had stood and killed a nice buck.

I remembered it had been raining too hard to leave the camp house until mid-morning. I remembered how discouraged I was because I had been unable to get to the camp in time to hunt the evening before, and then the rain had prevented the early morning hunt on Saturday. When the rain finally stopped, I had hunted the same way as this morning, had the altar prayer time and arrived at the same spot as today when the buck stepped out of the woods. He saw me as I saw him, and my first thought was, "He'll dash away into the woods before I can get my gun up." But I found him in the scope and squeezed the trigger, and he fell where he stood.

Now, two years later, I remembered my excitement when I saw the deer; but suddenly God carried me back to the events of the evening before in Camden. I remembered my disappointment when Rachel told me that her Sunday school class was taking turns carrying meals to the family of a terminally ill mother, Glenda Daily. Rachel's turn to take the meal would be Friday evening, so we would be unable to leave town early enough for me to make the late evening hunt.

"Why did you have to pick Friday?" was my question when she first told me of the mission.

"It just worked out that way," she said. So, somewhat dejected, I resolved that we would have to join Steve and his family at a later hour. I would miss what is usually the best time to get a deer.

Now, two years later as I stood in the road, I remembered something else that had happened when we took the supper to Glenda and her children. I told her we were on the way to the camp house to hunt. "I'll be praying for you," she said as we left.

When I saw Glenda again, she asked, "Did you kill a deer?" Suddenly I remembered the twinkle in Glenda's eye and the faint smile on her hurting face when I told her about the fine buck. It wasn't long after that before Glenda went to be with the Lord, but it took me two years to realize that the deer I had shot didn't happen there by chance. He was Glenda's deer, put there by the Lord.

I wonder how many times we enjoy something because someone prayed for us and God answered that prayer.

15

I Want to Be Part

"Ernie, I can't go with you on those lay revivals, but I want to be a part of the team. I can pray, so let me know the date of each one," said Mrs. Virginia Stuart, a senior member of the Camden Baptist Church.

"Miss ," as she is affectionately called by those who know her, has been and continues to be a pillar of spiritual strength to many people. At the time of this writing (January 1989), she is one of those I want praying for me when I have a special spiritual need. It was several years ago when she spoke to me after church one morning and requested to be part of the lay team. As I got to know Miss Virginia and recognized her dedication to the Lord's work, I've gone to her many times with my own prayer requests. One of those times was tonight.

I have been invited to speak at Deacon's Rallies in Birmingham and Montgomery during February, and I wanted to inform "Miss Virginia" to pray for me as I share some witnessing experiences. She is now well into her eighties but her mind is still sharp and clear, although she is in poor health and unable to come to church very often.

During our conversation, I remarked that Rachel and I were discussing our upcoming Sunday School lesson which deals with spiritual growth. "I have a list of things by which we can measure our spiritual growth," replied "Miss Virginia." "I was looking at it today. If you will wait a minute, I think I can find it."

I expected "Miss Virginia's" list would be worthwhile so I asked Rachel to copy it and share with her Sunday School class.

"I don't remember where I got these, but I get the list out every so often and check the ones I am weak in," added the saintly lady.

As I reviewed "Miss Virginia's" list, I couldn't see any places she would need to check. But I suppose that she, like all of us, has some weak spots; but I believe that her checks would be a lot fewer than mine.

About a year ago I received word at a deacon's meeting that her only son had died tragically. I hurried to the house and found "Miss Virginia" and her daughter-in-law in a state of shock. "This is the most difficult thing I have ever had to bear, but the Lord will help me through it," she said.

"Miss Virginia", widowed for many years, has had her share of difficulties. But she has never lost faith and has been a shining light for all who know her. Following is her list for measuring spiritual growth:

Evidence of Growing in Grace

1. Remaining joyful under crosses, disappointments and severe pain.
2. Growing jealousy for the honor of God and purity of His Church.
3. A growing deadness to the flattery or censorship of others.
4. Losing more and more consciousness of self.
5. Less temptation to resentment.
6. An increasing deadness to things the world has to offer.
7. Being less and less disposed to speak severely or to judge uncharitably of others.
8. A growing tranquillity under sudden and crushing disaster.

On Friday, February 1, 1991, Miss Virginia slipped away to be with the Lord. It was a trip she had wanted to make for a long time. But she had said she was willing to be here for as long as the Lord could use her. I think He used her until the very end.

About three weeks before her death, I went to her house, gave her some of the chapters of this book to read, including what I had written in this chapter. Then I asked that she pray for me and those who will attend a Deacon and Pastor's Association Rally at the Bethlehem Baptist Church in Headland. Miss Virginia commented that she couldn't pray as she once did (I think she meant hours rather than minutes as most of us pray), but she would remember the meeting.

"But, Ernie, always remember—it's not what I do, it's who I know that makes the difference," was her final comment as we parted at the door.

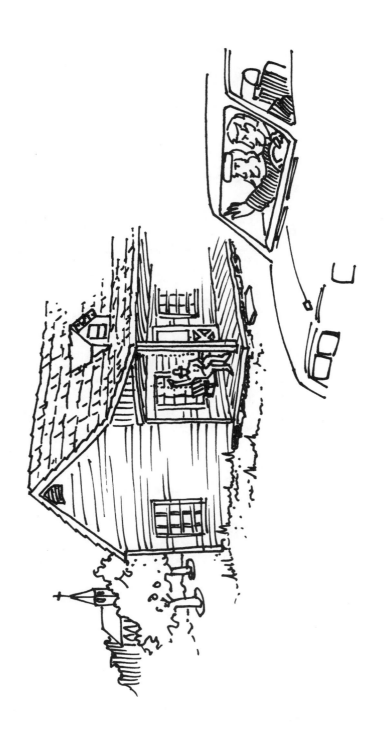

16

He Waved Every Sunday

And he said unto them, Go ye into all the world, and preach the gospel to every creature (Mark 16:15).

Most Christians are familiar with the "Great Commission" which Jesus gave to each of us as His disciples. We are further challenged to be His witnesses because of the promise of power. "I am with you always, even until the end of the world" (Matthew 28:20). I knew these Scriptures, but I wasn't doing much to carry out the Great Commission until the Lay Team came to Camden in 1975. Perhaps my apathy toward witnessing can be understood through the story of an old man whose home was one block from my church.

He lived in a corner house which fronted the street I traveled to and from church. There was a stop sign across the street from his house, and I began to notice him sitting in a swing as we made the stop each Sunday on our way to church. He began to recognize us as we stopped for the sign.

One day I waved and he immediately waved back. From then on we waved at each other every Sunday.

I wondered about the old man. I didn't think he was going to any of the churches, because most of them, like ours, had morning services. He was always right there in the swing, so he couldn't be attending.

The months turned into years as our family faithfully passed the house on our way to church. Unless the weather was unusually bad, the old man was always in the swing, and I could count on his hardy wave as we crossed the main street. If I ever thought about stopping and talking to him, I don't remember it—until the Lay Team came.

During that Lay-Led Revival, I caught a glimpse of personal witnessing and made a commitment to be a sharing Christian. One of my first assignments from the Lord was the man I had waved at for over three years.

I found out from a friend that he was a bachelor. "I don't think it will do much good to talk to him," said my friend. "I tried to witness to him, but he didn't want to listen."

My friend's words were not discouraging because the Lord had given me a new boldness following my commitment after the revival. So one afternoon Rachel and I parked on the street beside his house as he was leisurely moving to and fro in the swing. He knew who we were, and gave us a hearty welcome as we introduced ourselves and joined him on the porch.

It didn't take long to realize that he was a lonely

man who was enjoying our visit—until we began to talk about the Lord. His conversation then took on a tone of unbelief. "Charlie has been talking to me and said he has religion now. I told him all he has is 'Hot Religion.'"

"What's 'Hot Religion?'" I asked.

"That means it'll soon go away after it gets cold," he replied.

I tried to assure him that I felt Charlie, like myself, had made a sincere commitment to the Lord and wanted to share the love of Christ with him. He quickly changed the subject and would not let us talk about spiritual things any more that day. But the initial burden the Lord had given to both Rachel and me grew and he became an object of prayer and many visits in the months and years that followed.

If Rachel had cooked a special dish, she would often say, "Let's take our friend a portion." Once when my daddy was visiting, we brought him to the house for a meal. In spite of our friendship, it was quite a while before he would talk about the Lord. He was a master at changing the subject when we tried to witness. Once when I thought he was ready to listen, he interrupted in the middle of a sentence and asked me if I would like to have the cat that was on the porch. I often left his house thinking there was no hope for him. Then one afternoon he stopped swinging and made a statement which made me realize our witnessing was not in vain.

"My parents took me to church when I was a boy, but I quit going when I got older. After they died, the preacher came by to see me sometimes. He would talk about baseball, the weather, and a lot of other things, but he never asked me about my spiritual condition. I wonder why?" he asked. I couldn't answer his question, but I knew there was hope because of his deep thoughts about his spiritual condition.

In the meantime, the Lord sent David, a neighbor, to add his witness. David often came and read the Bible to him. And Charlie continued to be a regular witness when he went downtown. The old man watched Charlie and finally decided he didn't have "Hot Religion."

He no longer rejected witnessing as the Holy Spirit softened his heart. One day he told me about getting sick during the winter. "I passed out and fell on the floor. I couldn't get up and was there all night. I had a dream and thought I was about to go into hell, then I came to and was able to get back on the bed. I could feel the fire before I came to," he added.

I told him if he had Jesus, he wouldn't have to go there again. He responded with his standard reply, "Can't do it ,boy, can't do it."

I had heard that he had been quite a playboy in his young years, so one day I asked him if he thought he had lived too bad a life to be saved. "Maybe that's it," he said.

Winter came, and and one Wednesday night, for some reason, I was driving Rachel to choir practice. We can't remember why I did that, because she usually went alone. As we passed the old man's house, a police car and two other vehicles were beside his house. "Something must have happened to our friend," I said to Rachel. I quickly took her the one block to church and returned.

As I walked through the door, a man was saying, "You are not going to die."

"We are all going to die, but if we know Jesus, it will be all right," I said without introduction. The words seem to carry some kind of magic, because immediately everyone was gone, and the old man and I were alone.

I found out later that he had tried to check himself into the hospital, but they had sent him home with the help of the policeman. I had also heard that several years before, a sister who had an apartment in the same family home died suddenly while she was alone. I believe his near-death experience and the thought of dying alone motiv- ated the effort to get into the hospital. But whatever the reason, death was on his mind as I faced him that cold winter night.

"Would you like for me to read you some Scripture?" I asked.

After he consented, I took out my New Tes- tament and randomly opened it to the 14th chapter of John and began to read:

> In my Father's house are many mansions: if it were not so, I would have told you. I go to pre- pare a place for you. And if I go and prepare a place for you, I will come again, and receive you unto myself; that where I am, there ye may be also. And whither I go ye know, and the way ye know. Thomas said unto him, Lord, we know not

whither thou goest; and how can we know the way? Jesus said unto him, I am the way, the truth, and the life: no man cometh to the Father, but by me (John 14:2-6).

Somewhere within the chapter, I stopped reading and explained, "Jesus said He has prepared a room in His mansion for you. He has a sign with your name on it ready to place over the door if you will only believe and ask Him to forgive you."

He raised his downcast head and asked, "Do you think He has?"

"We just read it," I said. "The Word doesn't lie. Don't you want Jesus to forgive your sins and save you?"

"Yes, let's pray."

I led him in the sinner's prayer that night as he acknowledged Jesus as Savior. Rachel made a point to see him the next day and congratulate him on his victory in Jesus. A few weeks later, he was in one of the local stores when the Lord called him to claim his reservation.

It's been sixteen years now since this story had its beginning. I still pass by the house going to church. It's vacant now, but if someone moves in and I see them swinging on the porch during church hours, I hope the Lord, in His continuing reality, will give me grace to stop and visit.

17

The Tree That Wouldn't Fall

An old abandoned house, surrounded by several large trees, stood in the middle of a ten-acre field on the farm we purchased near Camden. I planted the field in pecan trees, tore down the house and one by one removed the old trees around the house. But the largest tree of all, a mammoth white oak almost five feet in diameter and over a hundred feet tall, still stood.

A hollow on one side was large enough for a man to walk inside and be protected from the elements. A shell, about a foot thick, extended around two-thirds of its trunk. Approximately ten feet up the tree branched into five trunks, or individual trees, which reached to the sky and branched evenly in every direction.

I knew that the tree, even for an experienced logger, would be dangerous to cut. I talked to various loggers about cutting it, but after hearing my description, no one ever had any time to do the job. I knew that its long root system was taking the water and nutrients from the pecan trees, so one beautiful Saturday I got out my chain saw and decided to cut it down.

Peter, a high school teenager who was working for me that day, cleared away the privet that grew at the tree's base. As I was about to send Peter away from the area, I said, "Peter, have prayer with me before you go."

I prayed and asked God to keep me safe while I cut the tree. Then for the first time since Peter had been helping me, it seemed right to talk to him about Jesus. Peter assured me he was saved, that he attended church regularly and had been baptized.

"The Bible says we should pray about everything," I told Peter. "He is as interested in our cutting this tree as He is in the other things we do," I said as I sent him back toward the house.

Glad that Peter was a Christian, I started my cut on the tree. It was easy to cut through the shell, as I cut first on one side of the hollow and then the other. After I cut a ways, I began to drive in wedges behind the cut so the tree would not lean backwards and bind the saw. I expected the tree to start its fall after I cut through the hollow, but its perfectly balanced top did not move. I kept cutting until there was only a splinter of hinge wood left, but there was still no movement. If I cut any more, the saw would definitely bind and the tree could roll off the stump in any direction. Whatever I did, I now had a first-class safety hazard for myself and anyone else who might come around the tree.

I knew that I couldn't saw anymore, so I began to think about my options. "If we just had a little wind, it would blow the tree down in a minute," I thought. In the meantime, it was dangerous to stay around the tree's base, so I went to the house and made some warning signs and placed them in the area — just in case someone came by and we didn't see them.

We ate lunch and there was still no wind. Neil, my son-in-law, was home, and he suggested we try to jack up one side. We tried that but the jack wasn't large enough. I talked to my neighbor who had a wrecker, but his cable wasn't long enough to keep the tree from falling on him. I thought about setting off a stick of dynamite in the hollow, but I couldn't locate any. Out of options, I finally decide that God was big enough to take care of the situation.

Sunday came and went without the calm being broken. Before I left for work on Monday morning, I asked Rachel to call if anything happened. At lunch time, she still hadn't called. I closed the office door and prayed, "Lord, please send the wind to blow the tree down; and God, please don't let it mash a single pecan tree." I had already prayed many times before, but this time it seemed God would answer. In a few minutes the phone rang and Rachel said the tree was down and not a single pecan tree was mashed. The few minutes was the time it took for her to go see if any of the pecans were mashed.

I think my lesson from this experience was that when we put things in God's hands through our prayers, He will take care of them. When I was frustrated before the tree fell, maybe He was saying, as He always says when we have problems, "Just trust me, I'll take care of it in due time."

18

An Opening

I met James Harold Kennedy, a reporter for the Birmingham News, in the early eighties. During his initial call to my place of employment, James said he wanted to write a story about MacMillan Bloedel's operation in Alabama and its economic contribution to Wilcox County. One of my jobs was to work with the news media, so we planned an interview date.

On the appointed day, James arrived early. I gave him information about the company, then we toured the plants and visited the the superior tree seed orchard before going to Camden for lunch.

James was a warm person and easy to talk to, but his physical appearance was somewhat frail. During the morning, I had the feeling that I should talk to him about Jesus. But no opening had come until we were about to finish lunch.

"James, I've had some serious health problems recently," I began as I was about to relate my near-death experience during the heart attack.

James interrupted, "I've had a lot of health problems, too; but I've found someone who can take care of them."

"Who?" I responded.

"Jesus Christ." With that answer, James took off with his personal testimony. For the next several minutes he told of his experience of getting to know Jesus in a personal way.

He told of going through two marriages, of becoming an alcoholic, of the horror of life as a police reporter and of feeling his life and health waste away until he almost had no hope. Following that background, James became more and more excited as he related the story of finding Jesus. He said it began through an ex-wife who had been saved after their marriage. She had told James of her experience and had encouraged him to come to Jesus; but James said he wasn't sure there even was a God at that time. But through her testimony, and because of his dying condition, he opened the door of a faint hope.

"In that condition, I opened myself to the Lord and He began to show me His reality. Instance after instance began to happen as the Lord revealed himself to me," said James.

"My former wife had quoted a verse of Scripture. I went home and turned on the TV set and Billy Graham was quoting the same verse. Similar events happened again and again until I knew that the recurrence was no accident. I knew that the Lord was real. I asked for salvation. I asked for new health. Christ gave me both.

"He didn't totally heal me overnight. But I no

longer had to take medications just to get to work the next day. The booze I had to have just to stay alive, I now no longer needed. Day by day my strength has returned. Yes, I know somebody that can take care of your health problems, Jesus Christ," restated James as we concluded our lunch.

James and I spent a lot of time that afternoon talking about what the Lord had done for us, rather than what MacMillan Bloedel was doing for the local economy. Oh, James returned to Birmingham and wrote a marvelous story about the company that gave us statewide recognition; but the day proved something of a relearning experience. Put the Lord first and He will produce more in a few minutes than we can hope to accomplish all day.

James and I became friends for life that day. I invited him to join our Lay Team and he became a regular participant, often taking vacation time to attend. I have heard him give his testimony many times. God has used him as a witness of His spiritual and healing power. I realize that the Lay Team was the real reason God put James and me together.

When we see each other at revivals, we often laugh about how we waited for the opening to talk about our Savior. But the Lord led James to use what I thought was going to be my opening. God does provide the opening and He does heal our health problems.

19

Remember the Sabbath Day

Remember the sabbath day, to keep it holy. Six days shalt thou labour, and do all thy work: But the seventh day is the sabbath of the Lord thy God: in it thou shall not do any work, thou, nor thy son, nor thy daughter, thy manservant, nor thy maidservant, nor thy cattle, nor thy stranger that is within thou gates: For in six days the Lord made heaven and earth, the sea, and all that in them is, and rested the seventh day: wherefore the Lord blessed the sabbath day, and hallowed it (Exod. 20:8-11).

It had been an unusually wet spring, but the sun was shining brightly when my family and I arrived at the Pine Flat Baptist Church on Sunday. I had been a member of this church, located in the Suttle community in Perry County, for almost eighteen years. During sixteen years as a vocational agriculture teacher, I had become acquainted with almost everyone there. Now that I was working for MacMillan Bloedel, I didn't get to see the people as often as when I was teaching, so it was good to get to church early and discuss the local news before the services began. A group of men were already on the grounds when I arrived.

"Your new company sure doesn't have much respect for the Sabbath," was the comment from one of the men as I joined the group.

"Why do you say that?" I asked.

"They have a logging crew just down the road running wide open," was his response.

His comment hit me by surprise. At that time I was employed in the Woodlands Division and attended the weekly staff meetings where many of the new decisions were made. Logging on Sunday had not been discussed.

I went to the logging location, stopped the crew, and asked why they were working. I found out that a supervisor had offered to give overtime pay if they volunteered to work. I didn't think the Sunday work had been set up through the local division manager, so I told the men to take a break until I got back.

The division manager, like myself, knew nothing about the Sunday logging. We reached a mutual agreement to shut the crew down, and I returned to the woods and sent them home.

Needless to say, logging on Sunday was our first subject at the weekly staff meeting the next morning. The log yard, which was almost empty because of all the wet weather, was part of the discussion. The supervisor who had sent the crew out had received the green light because of the shortage of logs. We talked at length about the need to keep the mill going as opposed to the poor public image we would create through Sunday logging.

My comment was, "There are jobs that have to be done on Sunday, but I don't think logging is one of them. God made the Sabbath day for worship and man's rest. If we don't honor God, He won't bless us."

"What we need is some dry weather, then we can log the mill," was the comment of the person in charge of procurement at that time. With that statement the discussion ended.

Almost two months later I was driving to work when the though hit me with a flash, "How long has it been since it rained?" Suddenly I realized how long it had been. We'd had to supply our skidder operators with dust masks and face shields so they could get in and out of the log landings. The log yards were full and we were back to five-day work weeks. I knew in that instant that God had withheld the rain and honored us because we had honored Him by not working on Sunday.

In the approximately twenty years that followed until I retired, the loggers never worked on Sunday again. We had our ups and downs with the log supply, but there was usually always enough to keep the mills going.

In this age of materialism, our society has gradually forgotten the fourth of the Ten Commandments: "Remember the sabbath day, to keep it holy." Stores that once closed on Sunday are now open seven days a week. Many employees cannot attend Sunday church services because of work requirements. Professing Christians shop on Sunday, the same as any other day. What will happen if the trend continues? Will God be pleased?

Since Jesus came and died for our sins, we are no longer under the law for salvation. "For by grace are ye saved through faith; and that not of yourselves: it is the gift of God: Not of works, lest any man should boast" (Ephesians 2: 8-9). But Jesus, in the Sermon on the Mount, made it quite clear that He did not come to destroy the law but to fulfill it (Matthew 5:17). In Romans 3:31 Paul said we do not void the law through faith but establish it.

I suppose the question is, "How do we keep the sabbath holy?" Jesus, in his compassion for people, did many things on the sabbath, including healing. He further said, "The sabbath was made for man, and not man for the sabbath" (Mark 2:27).

I don't pretend to know all the answers, but I believe He was talking about a day for His people to gather together for worship and rest. To me, its refreshing to be in the Lord's house with my Christian friends as we are inspired through spiritual music and the proclaimed Word. The afternoon rest may come in many ways. I've always liked the nap time, the slow walk through the woods, thoughts of last week, plans for the future—just relaxing and letting the Lord recharge my energy for the next week.

20

The Faith of a Child

(Recorded February 28, 1984)

Verily I say unto to you, Whosoever shall not receive the kingdom of God as a little child, he shall not enter therein (Mark 10:15).

I continue to be amazed at the faith of little children. Last week Diane, our daughter-in-law, related the kindergarten experience of Ashley, our granddaughter.

"Mama, my friend Gina (not her real name) cried at school today."

"What was she crying about?" Diane asked.

"She said she had to give her parents two valentines because they didn't live together anymore. She loves them both and she wishes her daddy would come back home. I told her she should pray and ask God to bring them back together again. Gina said she was going to pray and ask God to do that," said Ashley.

Diane said her comment to Ashley was, "That was real sweet."

A few days later Ashley came home and was casually discussing the school day with her mother. "And, mama, Gina said her daddy came to the house last night, and she heard him and her mother talking in the kitchen. Her daddy said he was coming home and he and her mother plan to get married again."

Suffer little children to come unto me, and forbid them not, for of such is the kingdom of God (Mark 10:14).

21

A Castaway Named Bill

In everything give thanks: for this is the will of God in Christ Jesus concerning you (1 Thess. 5:18).

Just as my daddy had during his lifetime, I had always owned a bird dog. But mine had died suddenly and I had been searching for another so I could hunt birds after deer season went out in late January. During the Christmas holidays I had mentioned the need for a dog to my brother-in-law, Wayne Dubose, who lives in Atlanta, Georgia.

"A neighbor of mine has a pointer he wants to get rid of," said Wayne. " If he still has the dog, I'll bring it my next trip. It's a well-bred dog, but the owner moved from a rural place in Mississippi and has decided he can't keep it in the city," he added.

Wayne brought the beautiful young dog the last of deer season. During our first outing on Sunday afternoon, which was nothing more than a walk around the lake, the dog ran well. Maybe a little too rangy, but nothing that couldn't be corrected. He seemed to be the perfect answer to my prayer, and I thanked God for him several times that day.

On Monday afternoon when I got home from work, I heard dogs barking in the woods below the lake. Their tone let me know immediately that they were in the excitement of a chase. As I stepped from my car I saw four deer break from the woods and bound across the corn field, headed for the Alabama River swamp about a mile from our house. The lead dog, close behind the deer, was my new bird dog and was being closely followed by our two beagles. Soon they were out of hearing. I looked at the dog pen where they were supposed to be and saw a wide open gate. Rachel explained later that she had gone to feed the dogs and they had bounded by her when she opened the gate.

One of the beagles returned that night and the other the next day. The bird dog, which had a collar but no name tag, never was seen again.

I couldn't understand the turn of events, especially since I had seen the dog as an answer to prayer and had been faithful to thank God for him. I related the lost dog story at our deacon's meeting and Don McMillan, a fellow deacon, said, "A bird dog took up at my house. I know where he came from. As a matter of fact, his owner has cast him away and no longer wants him. He may get run over by a car in town, so you can have him if you want him," offered Don.

"Are you sure he is a bird dog?" I asked.

"Well, I don't know much about bird dogs, but I see him pointing sparrows in the back yard," answered Don.

That did it. If a dog will point sparrows, he will also point quail so I arranged a time to pick up the dog.

Life is full of mental images. We form an image of a person we talk to on the phone but have never met. Then when we meet the person, he or she is entirely different from our expectations. I had formed an image of my new dog. But the dog Don's children brought into the house was far from the image I had created in my mind. Never have I been so disappointed in a dog as I was that night. He looked like anything but a bird dog. His chin was square instead of pointed. Long hair protruded from the sides of his mouth, which gave him more the appearance of a schnauzer. Only his body, covered with long hair, gave him a slight appearance of a setter bird dog.

I had made a commitment, so I had to take the dog. But as I left, I said to Don, "If he doesn't work out, can I bring him back?"

I took him home to the country and named him "Bill." He was a congenial dog and we struck a good relationship. As we walked around the lake, he responded to my commands. He moved well, but I wondered if he could smell a quail, being at best only a half breed.

Two weeks later Steve and I drove to the farm in Suttle where we had lots of quail. The timber had been clear-cut two years before, leaving only a few hardwoods along the bottoms. The logging slash had been pushed in long wind rows which had grown up in briers, making ideal cover for quail. The hills and old fields were covered with many seed-bearing plants, which furnish excellent habitat for birds. The 280 acres had at least fifteen coveys of birds.

We arrived early and started at the high field where a covey usually stayed. Bill began hunting fifty yards ahead. He had hardly started when a large covey took to the air. Bill never slowed his pace and seemed to pay the birds no attention. "We really have a lemon," I said to Steve. "Let's go down to the bottom, maybe we can walk up some singles and get a shot," I suggested as I thought how foolish I had been to drive sixty miles to hunt with a cur dog.

We walked to the wind row at the bottom of the hill where we had seen the birds settle. Steve got on one side and I got on the other. I was surprised to see Bill get right into the thick briers as he gave the appearance of hunting birds. Suddenly out flew a bird on Steve's side. He nailed him with his second shot. Bill flushed another one which I dropped. In short order we had four more.

Bill wasn't pointing the birds the way a good dog is supposed to, but with his long hair for protection, he was getting in the briers and flushing the birds out. Then Bill found a dead bird, and for the first time ever, his part-bird-dog instinct took charge. He locked all four wheels as he froze in a point with his mouth a few inches from the bird. He soon broke the point and picked up the bird. I began to urge him to bring the bird. "Fetch, Bill, fetch."

To my surprise he brought the bird as if he had been doing it all his life. I gave Bill several pats on the head, the best reward I knew to give.

We went a little farther up the bottom and Bill froze again. This time it was a live bird. We made a clean shot and Bill saw the bird fall. Again I gave the command, "Fetch." Bill had learned quickly. He knew what I meant and soon had the bird for his second "pat on the head."

Bill got better and better that day and was pointing coveys of birds as well as singles. He wasn't perfect. He never got perfect. But Steve and I killed our limit and went back the next Saturday, the last day of the season, and killed fourteen more.

We enjoyed Bill for several seasons before he died. We could not only kill quail with him, but he was also a good dove retriever. He was easy to handle and keep up with. He was my kind of dog.

I have thought about Bill and the pointer many times, and have related the story on several speaking occasions. I don't know why it occurred, but I think God knew what I needed better than I. Maybe it was because I was thankful for the pointer and he gave me something better.

Maybe it was to show me that Bill was like people. On the outside he didn't look like much, but on the inside, he was something special. I wonder how many people I have been guilty of writing off as not being special on the inside.

22

No Coincidences

One of the highlights of my Christian walk has been to watch new believers share with others. I've come to recognize the old adage, "God doesn't want our ability, He wants our availability." Some of the most effective witnessing I have observed is by "babes in Christ", telling of the power of the Lord as He gave them assurance of eternal life.

I think it is their genuine sincerity, as they relate the freshness of their new found relationship with Jesus, that touches the hearts of unbelievers. One such person who began to share with those God puts in front of him after he was saved is Phillip Sims.

Phillip grew up in the nearby town of Pine Hill. He met Donna Jackson, a pretty young lady who often visited our Sunday School Couples Class with friends when she was home from college. Phillip had his eye on Donna and usually came with her. He seldom said anything in class, but I could tell that she was his reason for being there. Phillip's persistence paid off, and the couple was married after Donna received an engineering degree from the University of Alabama. They were both employed in the area, built a home on the river near Camden and became faithful members of the Couples Class.

Donna was very vocal in class participation, but Phillip still didn't have much to say. One year I asked each class member to write down their conversion experience and share it with someone else, and then later, as time permitted, be prepared to share it with the group. Most of the class participated, including Phillip.

Our church held a revival not long afterward, and God convicted Phillip that he was not saved. Phillip responded to the urging of the Holy Spirit, went forward, made a public profession of Jesus as Lord and Savior and asked for believers' baptism. The Lord began to make a morally fine, young man into a new creature after that commitment. No longer was he silent during class discussions. But more importantly, he shared Jesus wherever he went.

Each Sunday we devoted some class time to sharing weekly blessings. Phillip usually had something fresh to share. On December 20, 1985, I wrote in my notes the following events he had just shared:

"Donna and I were invited to a Christmas party which was to start Thursday evening at 7:00 P.M. I planned to leave our sales office in Thomasville no later than 5:00 P.M. so I could drive home in time to go. But a man whom I vaguely knew called fifteen minutes before quitting time and wanted to talk to me, so I said I would wait. It was almost five o'clock when he arrived. We did our business, and I was trying to conclude the conversation when he told me he was an alcoholic. Then it occurred to me, "God wants me to tell him about Jesus." I resolved I would stay until it opened for me to talk.

"He told me of losing his former job, and then his wife, because of alcohol. 'But I am going to AA now,' he said. 'And I hope things are going to be better.'"

"It was then I told him of my recent conversion, how I found the Lord and what He had done in my life," said Phillip.

"He said in AA they talked about a higher power and he believed God must be real. I encouraged him to go to church in Clinton, Misissippi, where he had just moved, read his Bible and seek God, who would help him.

"When we finished talking, I still made it home in time for us to get to the party. We ate at a table with Will and Beth Philpott, and I felt impressed to share the story with them. Will said he had a cousin who lived in Clinton. He would ask him to go see the man and invite him to his church.

"I was amazed at how the Lord worked to put us with Will," said Phillip. "He sure ties things together."

Betty Henderson, a dynamic, sharing Christian who had a conversation similar to Phillip's said, "There are no coincidences with the Lord."

23

Putting Out the Fleece

There are many dedicated, God-called preachers in this world and it always warms my heart to get to know one on a personal basis. A special addition to my circle of friends was Brother John H. Finklea Jr., pastor of the First Baptist Church of Brewton, Alabama.

Rachel and I were part of a Lay Team of eighteen people who worked with Brother John's church on July 12-16, 1989. It was during those five days that we got to know Brother John and his pretty wife, Delores, both special disciples of the Lord.

While sharing his testimony with the Lay Team, Brother Finklea stated that he had been raised in neighboring Monroe County, played some college football, married Delores, his high school sweetheart, and had good employment when God called him into the ministry. Thirteen years prior he had been very happy pastoring a lively church in Dansville, Virginia, when he was contacted by a pulpit committee from the First Baptist Church of Brewton.

"I told them I was very happy where I was and I didn't think they should pursue the matter with me when they called by phone. But they didn't listen and chartered a plane to come and hear me preach. I still had no desire to come to Brewton, in spite of their interest. But I was having some eye problems at the time. I couldn't focus my left eye. I couldn't tell who the people were on the first row of pews at church and a large spot was always in front of the eye.

"I went to a doctor and he said I had a detached retina, which might be corrected by taking my eye out and fusing the retina back together with a laser beam. But there was no guarantee that the operation would work, and I might lose the sight of that eye.

"When I am faced with a decision, I try to make sure that I am guided by the Lord. I still didn't think the Lord was interested in my going to Brewton, but I put the fleece out. 'Lord, if you want me to go to Brewton, heal my eye,' was the prayer I prayed before going to bed one night.

"The next morning as I went to shave, I noticed that the spot before my eye was gone. I quickly picked up a book. All the lines were in focus. I looked in the distance. Everything lined up perfectly. I found Delores and said, 'Honey, start packing, we're going to Brewton.' That was thirteen years ago, and God has blessed us many times over as we have sought to serve Him in this place," concluded Brother Finklea.

I saw some of the ways that God has blessed

Brother John during the week as he exercised his gifts, not only as a preacher but also as a one-on-one witness. As we visited, I had the privilege of meeting some older men who had recently come to Jesus and are now on fire for the Lord. Brother John confided with me, "God has given me a gift to share with men." I saw some of the results of that gift as our Lord was doing some wonderful work in the lives of those men who had come to know Him.

The Brewton Lay Revival was one of the best I have ever had the privilege of attending. Perhaps it was because of the sweet spirit and prayers of the church. When the fellowship of a church pray and ask God for revival, He hears.

George "Buster" Rogers, a pharmacist from Huntsville, was one of the speakers who shared his testimony during the opening Wednesday night service. "Buster" told how he ran from the Lord for a long time as a young man. But one night, while attending a revival service, he heard the Lord say that if he didn't make a decision for Him that night, He would not call him again.

"I still didn't go forward during the church invitation," said "Buster." "I went home, but again the Lord impressed me that His last call was that day. Finally, I knew I needed to act, so I got dressed and walked to the preacher's house. I told him how I felt, and in his living room I invited Christ into my heart. My life hasn't been the same since."

One thing I've learned about Lay Revivals is that God knows who should share at each service. Usually we don't know who will share until our prayer time when the coordinator calls upon whom he feels are to be the speakers.

A young man came forward during the invitation and verified that "Buster's" testimony spoke to his heart. He said he had been like "Buster," running from the Lord. But tonight he felt God wouldn't deal with him forever and he wanted to make Jesus his Lord.

God used that commitment as a catalyst to lead many others to make commitments during the week. The climax came on Saturday night. Harold Swearingen, revival coordinator, asked Yvonne Thaxton and Peyton Burford to share. Just as it had been throughout the week, the Holy Spirit touched Yvonne and the Lord used her testimony to move many people to come forward during the invitation. Harold felt led to give after Yvonne spoke.

In her testimony, Yvonne told of growing up in the Catholic Church, then marrying at a young age. The marriage lasted only a short time. Then she felt rejection from her church and dropped out of its activities. A few years later she met Kent Thaxton, a former professional baseball player and movie actor at the time. They married and moved back to his home state of Florida where Kent took a job with a large building supply chain.

Although Kent had attended church as a youth, he too had dropped out of church. While sharing his testimony to the Brewton church on Friday night, Kent said that things went well with the job and their marriage for a while. He became manager of a store and their son was born. But materialism was a major goal, and even though he had everything a person could want, things sometimes got bad. When they did, because of their upbringing, he and Yvonne turned to the church for a while, but then would slip back into the old ruts.

The pastor of the church where the Thaxtons occasionally attended visited one night. Kent said, "One by one, I showed him all my guns, rods, reels, boats, motors and other things I owned. I had one more boat motor and was off to show that when I suddenly stopped and said, 'Why am I running from the Lord?'

"The pastor took me back to the kitchen table and presented the plan of salvation. I prayed to receive Christ that night and He has been real to me ever since," shared Kent during his Friday night testimony.

When Yvonne spoke Saturday, she said, "I prayed the same prayer that Kent prayed that night, but nothing happened in my life as it did in his. Kent started going on Lay Revivals. The first one was at Panama City Beach. He came back excited and tried to tell me what the Lord had done, but I didn't want to hear about it. He went to other places. Always it was the same. Kent and his mountain-top experiences and me trying to put on a front, but not really wanting to hear what happened.

"Then I decided what I really needed to do was get busy in the church. I became a Sunday School teacher but my frustrations continued. I was miserable.

"One morning at breakfast I told Kent I was going shopping at the mall. I needed some money, which he promised to give me if I would come by the store where he could cash a check. When I arrived at the store, Kent waited and waited before he finally brought out the money. As he handed it to me he said, 'I made you an appointment with our pastor. Go by and talk to him before you go shopping.'

"I was enraged. 'I don't need to see the pastor. I'm not going. You can call him back and cancel the appointment because I'm going shopping,' I cried out as I drove away. I didn't know until later that Kent had confided to the pastor that I was under conviction.

"My memory is hazy about getting there, but at the appointed time I found myself outside the pastor's study. He invited me in and we talked about the Lordship of Jesus. The pastor, Brother David Shofner, has written a book titled Soul Winning, in which he uses one verse of Scripture to explain salvation: Romans 10:13, For whosoever shall call upon the name of the Lord shall be saved. Brother Shofner said that to be saved I had to make Jesus Lord of my life, that I could no longer be Lord.

"Before, when I had prayed, I hadn't made Jesus Lord. That day I made Him Lord and He saved me. I was no longer on the throne of my life. For the first time, I was willing to give Jesus complete control. In that moment I knew I belonged to Jesus."

The Holy Spirit continued to speak through Yvonne as she shared highlights of their new family and church life.

The invitation was very touching as person after person came to speak to Brother Finklea and make commitments to the Lord. When the service was finally closed, people didn't want to go home. They stood around in small groups sharing the excitement of the Lord. People made commitments following the other services, but Saturday night was a special night I shall always remember.

I've heard that a valid evaluation of a revival can only be made a year later. But the real results won't be known until we are in heaven. I wonder about the young man in a trailer park who had just arrived from Louisiana in an overheated car. Even though he didn't make a decision then, will he come to Christ now that he knows God's plan for his salvation? Or the truck driver who came over to let us know that the folks we were looking for were not home? Or a next door neighbor whom God had home at the right time to hear a lay person's testimony of Christ's love for him? Or the man in the hospital who would never listen to anyone until he was flat on his back? On and on the list could go of contacts that were made by the team and church members during the week. What will the results be?

Only God knows the answer. Our job is to go and tell the good news of the Gospel in a spirit of love and compassion for the lost of this troubled world.

Brother Finklea, in a follow-up letter to the visiting team members, writes about the rewards we get for telling people about Jesus:

"...Our Lord truly did a wonderful work in the lives of all of us during these days.

"I wish you could have heard those who shared in the Sunday evening service. It was great to hear them say what Jesus means to them and how they had been convicted to share Him wherever they go. We had many more decisions on Sunday night.

"All across my years as a pastor, my heart has been sharing Christ on a one-to-one basis. I have taught that we are rewarded by our obedience to go and share, and that reward was truly great this past week."

It was indeed a great earthly reward to be a member of the revival team and have fellowship in the home of a precious couple, Harold and Loraine Burns.

24

Children in Trouble

It was a Sunday afternoon. I was dozing on the couch after reading the paper. Suddenly a strange feeling came over me. My daughter Denise came to mind and with her image came the thought that she was in some kind of trouble.

"Denise is in trouble and we need to pray for her," I said to Rachel as we both quickly awakened from our drowsiness. I got on my knees and asked God to take care of her, to meet her needs whatever they were.

When Steve, and later Denise, had gone to college, we had turned them over to the Lord for His safe keeping. We mentioned them almost daily in our prayers, but I felt this unction of the Holy Spirit was for a special need.

When we contacted Denise, she told us that she and some friends had gone bowling that Sunday afternoon. As she was bowling, her vision suddenly became blurred and she had a tremendous headache and was on the verge of blacking out. But just as quickly as the problem had come, it went away. I'm convinced that the Lord took the problem away as soon as we prayed. Two other experiences I have heard about reinforce this belief.

The first is the testimony of Barry Barrett, an American Airlines pilot from Tennessee. Barry, while sharing at a Lay Revival, said he was a pilot in the Navy following World War II and was doing a tour of duty at the South Pole. One day his plane was the radio contact for a flight of helicopters that were taking scientists to explore the countryside several miles from their base.

"As each helicopter completed his mission, I checked it off, until they were all headed for home base. My seven passengers and I made our final turn and also headed for the base. We had hardly started when one of the engines froze up and died. In a few minutes the other began to shake and vibrate. The only way I could stop the vibration was to head the plane straight down and pick up an enormous amount of air speed. But the minute I picked the nose up to keep from hitting the mountains that old plane would shudder and fall again. We fell out of the sky like a leaf in the autumn wind. I switched all the switches and did all the emergency procedures I had been taught to do. But nothing stopped the vibration.

"I didn't have time to get a radio call off to home base. At about eighteen-hundred feet, the engine froze up with a loud noise. Around eleven-hundred feet, we broke out of the clouds in a steep dive headed straight down toward the ground. I managed to pull the airplane wings level and belly it into the snow as we slid several feet. It was a hard landing, but nobody got hurt.

"It was thirty-eight degrees below zero when we crawled out. In front of the plane was nothing but flat snow. But behind the plane, about one hundred yards away, the mountains went straight up, right into the clouds. We didn't miss them much.

"We heard a helicopter coming along the base of the mountain. Apparently, he was the last one that had called in. The sound got louder, then faded away and he was gone. Our hearts fell and we figured we might be there forever. We would not be the first to die at the South Pole and not be found until years later. All of a sudden, we began to hear the sound of a helicopter again. It got louder and louder as it dropped to pick us up and take us back to the base. A scientist riding in the back seat had told the pilot he thought he saw something, so they came back.

"About two weeks later, I went up in the mountains and got on the ham radio set to call home. The operator got a fellow in Montana and he relayed the call to my mom in Tennessee. In a very excited voice she said, "How are you?"

I said, "I'm fine, mom. I'm fine." That wasn't good enough, so she asked me a second time just to make sure I was all right.

"We have heard from your brother, and we have heard from your sister, but we haven't heard from you in over two weeks."

"I found out later that at two o'clock in the morning, my mother woke out of a deep sleep. She sat up in bed and reached over and shook my dad. She said, "Wake up, one of our children is in trouble, and we have to pray for them." They got out of their bed and on their knees and prayed for one of their children they thought was in trouble.

"There has never been any doubt in my mind that the minute that airplane engine froze, is the minute God answered my mother's prayer. I have also never doubted that two o'clock in the morning on that little old rocky farm in Tennessee is the middle of the afternoon at the South Pole."

Barry concluded his testimony about God communicating with his mother during his time of need by saying, "I don't know your life tonight. I don't know your needs. Your life may be vibrating and falling apart just like that old plane. Everything may be falling out from under you. Your marriage may be falling apart. But the same God who answered my mother's prayer from that little farm in Tennessee, across oceans and continents to the bottom of the world, can answer your prayer tonight. He is the same one who can give you eternal life if you don't know Him and are willing to accept Him as your Lord and Savior."

The second experience about God communicating with a parent when a child was in trouble was related to me a few weeks ago by Aubrey Spader of Baldwin County, Alabama. The event is very similar to Barry's.

Aubrey and I both attended Robertsdale High School, but we hadn't seen each other for years when I contacted his company about a used pecan shaker. He knew where one was for sale, so we set a date to get together.

144

On the appointed day, we talked about high school days and mutual friends as we drove to south Baldwin County to see the shaker. When the Lord gave the opening, I shared my personal testimony, which led Aubrey to share his. He told me that he had once been an Oliver Tractor and Equipment dealer. One winter the Oliver people invited dealers to tour their factory in Charles City, Iowa. Arrangements were made for the group to travel on a charter plane.

As Aubrey shared about the trip, he paused to tell me about his Christian mother. "I had built my house near my mother's, and I saw her almost every day. My mother was one of the most devout Christians I have ever known. At one time I had a heart problem and my doctor told me that by-pass surgery was an absolute necessity. Although I wasn't looking forward to it, I was making plans to check into the hospital when I told my mother. The next time I saw her she informed me that I didn't need the surgery. I could have it if I wanted to, but she didn't think I needed it.

"She sounded so convincing that I decided to wait. Weeks later I went back for a checkup with my doctor. He would hardly speak to me when I told him I didn't check in the hospital for the bypass operation. But when he examined me, he was amazed at my new condition. I know it was my mother's prayer.

"I told my mother good-by when I went on the Oliver Tractor Dealer tour. It was a nice trip. But when we started home, I noticed ice beginning to form on the plane's wing just outside my window.

The farther we went, the thicker it got. Then the pilot came on the speaker and said that the de-icer wasn't working and we were going to change altitudes. We all were real concerned about what was going to happen to the plane. It would shake like it was coming apart as we lost altitude. I knew enough about flying to know that if the ice build-up continued, a wing could just break off the plane. But the plane held together and we were able to land safely in Memphis, Tennessee at 1:00 A.M.

"I spent the rest of the night in Memphis and rode another plane home the next day. When I got home, I spoke to my mother before seeing anyone else. Her first words were, 'What were you doing at 11:00 P.M. last night?'

"'Why, mother?' I asked.

"'Something woke me up at 11:00 P.M. and I felt I heard the words: Aubrey is in trouble. I didn't know what the trouble was, only that you needed some help, so I started praying. I prayed and asked the Lord to help you until I felt you were all right,' was her comment as she began to ask me more about the trip."

Many other parents can probably share similar experiences about how God communicated with them when their offspring had special needs. To me, these three experiences not only reaffirm that God knows every happening on the face of this earth; but they also confirm the power of prayer by His people.

25

So Little to Offer

Henceforth there is laid up for me a crown of righteousness, which the Lord, the righteous judge , shall give me at that day: and not to me only, but unto all them also that love his appearing (2 Tim. 4:8).

I met Henry and Lois Waren at the Panama City Beach Baptist Church in Florida where we were holding a Lay-Led Revival. The couple had lived most of their life in Birmingham before buying a retirement home at the beach. They visited with the team every day and became regular team members for revivals that followed. I first heard Henry give his testimony several months later at the Farmstead Baptist Church in Jasper, Alabama, during a Lay Revival.

Henry was the first speaker on the opening Wednesday night service. "I've never done this before, and I don't mind telling you I'm about as nervous as a man can be," said Henry during his initial remarks. But the anointing power of the Holy

Spirit took over and led Henry to make a beautiful presentation.

Henry told how he was up in years before he found a personal relationship with Jesus. He gave a lot of credit to his wife for her prayers and witness, which led to his salvation experience.

Henry became an active participant in his church's visitation program. "My visiting partner and I almost wore one old man out. We visited him every week. We didn't talk about the Lord, we just visited," was Henry's comment. Henry then shared about going with his wife to a witnessing seminar where he began to learn to share Jesus.

Along the way Henry developed a heart condition and had to have open heart surgery. As he related his experience during the surgery, every person in the audience was touched. "I don't know if I died, or had a dream, or something else. I just know that I was with the Lord. I didn't see His face, but I was in His presence. But what I remember most was how I felt. I was so ashamed because I had so little to offer," shared Henry as he cupped one hand to illustrate the little he was bringing.

"As I stood shamefully before the Lord, His voice spoke to me and said, 'I'm not ready for you Henry. Go on back.'"

Henry told the people at Farmstead of his commitment to serve the Lord as he completed his testimony. He was faithful to that commitment in the approximately five years I knew him. He and Lois not only worked with our Lay Team, but a couple of other teams as well, often traveling many miles into other states. In the fall of 1987, they drove to Fayetteville, North Carolina. I last saw Henry alive at another Lay-Led Revival in Brewton, Alabama, the following month.

In Lay-Led Revivals and in his own church community, Henry used his opportunities to be about the Lord's business of sharing His good news for man. God gave Henry a gift of humor which was interwoven in his testimony and he became an excellent speaker. But I think Henry's real message was in making everyone who heard him examine their own "Gifts to the Master" as he related his near-death experience.

Henry had to have surgery again. He lapsed into a coma for about a month, then went to be with the Lord. This time he did not come back.

Rachel and I went to the funeral in Pell City, Alabama. We rode with Barry Barrett, an American Airlines pilot and sometimes coordinator of Lay-Led Revivals, to the burial site about twenty-five miles from town. Barry related that Henry and Lois had attended a revival in Columbia, Tennessee, shortly before the surgery. "The Lord impressed me to ask Henry to be the speaker for the closing service on Sunday morning. God blessed Henry that day. After he spoke, seven people accepted Jesus and were saved," said Barry.

We get to heaven by trusting in Jesus and accepting what He has done for us on the cross and not by righteousness or good deeds; but I don't believe that Henry was ashamed of his offering the second time he was before the Lord.

26

More Powerful Than a Two-Edged Sword

June 24, 1985

Last Monday night Jimmy Simpkins and I made a visit to the Wilcox County Jail to share Christ. Jimmy spoke to groups that were in individual cells and I spoke to those in the "bull ring," a large, double compartment cell with a long table in the front and tiered cots in the back.

God led me to share the story of Paul and Silas from the 16th chapter of Acts. I told of their missionary work in Philippi; of the slave girl who had fortune-telling ability because she was possessed with a demon; of Paul's mercy in casting out the demon; of the reaction of those who had benefited from her fortune telling because they lost their way of making money; and of how they stirred up the people and had Paul and Silas unjustly beaten and thrown into jail.

I told the seven men that if two people ever had a reason, from an earthly standpoint, to quit their missionary work—Paul and Silas did! They could have said, "Lord, we've been trying to serve you, but you have let us get beaten up and thrown in jail, so we quit right now." But instead, the Bible says they sang praises to the Lord and all the other prisoners heard them.

As I began to talk to the men, God's spirit was moving, but one man soon left the front and went into the back compartment and sat down on the edge of a bunk. I could see rejection written on his face.

I finished the story of Paul and Silas and the salvation of the Philippian jailer after he witnessed the power of God in setting the prisoners free. I told of Joseph and his unjust jail sentence. I related how he made the best of each situation as he spent his time in jail. I told of Joseph's interpretation of the dreams of Pharoah's butler and baker after he noticed their sad faces and tried to minister to them.

Like the butler and baker, the faces I was seeing before me were sad faces. I challenged each man to make a deal with me, if they believed it was reasonable, after hearing my proposal. They agreed—if they thought it was reasonable.

I told them, "Tomorrow, find the most discouraged person in jail and do something to encourage him, or write a letter home to a family member or friend. Pray about it and do what God leads you to do. Just make the best of your situation."

When I asked for a show of hands of those who thought the request was reasonable and would accept the challenge, the man who had left the room and was sitting on the bunk was the first to raise his hand. God's Word is more powerful than a two-edged sword.

27

Be Not Weary in Well Doing

(Recorded March 12, 1984)

Let us not be weary in well doing; for in due season we shall reap, if we faint not (Gal. 6:9).

God doesn't ask us to witness to everybody, but He does ask us to witness to somebody. One of the somebodies God gave me was a rough-talking neighbor.

Shortly after I met him, he became ill and most of the time was bedridden. I visited him on a fairly regular basis. He liked to talk but invariably would end up lambasting someone—a neighbor, public official, church group, etc.

When I would bring up the Lord, he would evade the question and I would leave thinking that my witness had made no impression. But he usually consented to having prayer before I left and his "thank you" kept me going back.

One day I asked him point blank if he was a

Christian. "Calvin, will you go to heaven when you die?" He answered yes, but was soon giving a neighbor's reputation a hard time. There was no fruit in his life.

During a Lay Revival at our church, I took Henry McElroy, another layman, to see Calvin. Henry talked about eternal assurance and asked Calvin about his assurance.

Calvin was unsure of where he would spend eternity and finally admitted that he didn't guess he really had Christ in his heart. Henry read the Scriptures and led Calvin to receive Christ.

About a year later, my neighbor died. As I talked with his widow, she said, "Calvin started to change that day, and I know he's in heaven now."

I thought of the times I had visited Calvin and had left his house discouraged about the witness. But God promises that His Word will not return to Him as void, so let us not be weary in well doing.

28

Being Part of Happy Things

...Eye hath not seen, nor ear heard, neither have it entered into the heart of man, the things which God hath prepared for them that love him (1 Cor. 2:9).

In January of 1986, I attended a basketball game at our local high school. I was talking to a friend, Peyton Burford, when he pointed out a young man who was home for the Christmas holidays. "That's Ewing Fuller, who is now attending Texas A & M University. He had leukemia but has had a miraculous healing," said Peyton.

I hadn't know Ewing personally, but I had met his parents several years ago when we lived in the Hybart community near his home in Vredenburgh. I knew that Ewing had been at the point of death and recalled that a fund had been established at a Camden bank to help with his hospital expenses. I had also heard that he, like myself, had experienced a "near-death" spiritual journey, so I wanted to compare notes.

I moved to the vacant seat by Ewing and introduced myself. After some light talk, I asked about his recovery.

"I have been cured," said Ewing as he gave praise to the Lord.

As we talked, I related my own near-death experience when I had the heart attack in 1974. I told Ewing of feeling that my spirit had left my body and that I had heard the music of heaven. I asked him if he had a similar experience.

"On one occasion, I was in a corner of the hospital room watching a nurse changing the IV in the arm of a patient. As I watched, I realized it was me lying on the hospital bed and not someone else. Another time, I was in the presence of a light, and I knew it was the Lord. Then it seemed as if I became a part of the light," explained Ewing.

I asked Ewing if he heard music during those times. "I can't say that I remember hearing music. What I remember most was the joy of being part of happy things. One thing I learned is that dying is not an experience to dread," smiled Ewing.

Ewing and I agreed that if a person has Jesus in his heart, everything is going to be all right on the other side. But until that time comes, we each have a purpose here on earth.

29

Guardian Angels

*He that dwelleth in the secret place of the most High
shall abide under the shadow of the Almighty...For he
shall give his angels charge over thee, to keep thee in all
thy ways. They shall bear thee up in their hands, lest
thou dash thy foot against a stone (Ps. 91:1,11,12).*

God and His angels are mentioned throughout
the Bible. Our present pastor, Eddie Davidson,
recently said that sometimes the angels of the Bible
were God himself. I'm convinced that we have a
protector, whether it's God or an assigned angel,
to always take care of us when we trust and seek
His security. I have already mentioned some close
calls; another experience of God's protection and
reality came about on January 31, 1988.

Rachel wanted some of the scrub oak trees
which were overhanging her flower border cut
because they shaded its growth. Neil and Denise
were visiting for the week end and Neil volunteered
to help with the job. After we finished cutting the

oak trees, I noticed that a pine, perhaps eighty feet tall, had a bad fusiform rust scar. Because of the defect, it could easily break and fall on the house if we had a strong west wind. I decided it also should be cut.

Cutting trees, especially large ones, is always dangerous. So I prayed for protection before we brought the tractor and tied a long rope to the tree so we could pull it away from the house as it was being felled. Every thing went well and the tree was soon on the ground as we had planned.

The last tree to be cut was another scrubby top pine. I looked it over for widow makers (dead limbs that might fall and make someone else a widow), saw none, and soon had it on the ground.

Neil and I, standing almost side by side, were admiring our work when suddenly a large pine limb, falling like a giant spear, embedded itself in the ground between us. It had evidently broken from the larger pine when it rolled against a tall oak as it was falling. The limb had then remained in the oak until the job was finished, only to fall by the light wind action.

The sharp point of the limb would have probably killed either of us if it had made a direct hit. God, or His angel, does looks after us— especially when we take time to pray.

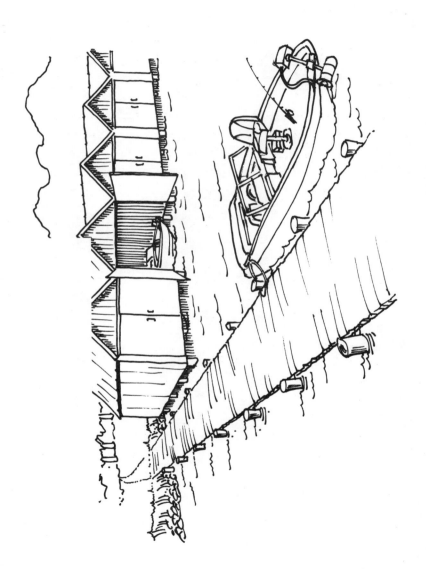

30

The Fishing Club

Follow me and I will make you fishers of men (Matt.
4:19).

On the Monday night after Christmas I had
invited my son, Steve, to speak to the Camden
Work Release Prisoners during our weekly Bible
study. He was to be home for the Christmas
holidays, and I thought it would be a good
opportunity for him to share the spiritual experience
he had in his church during their fall revival.
However, he had stopped in Selma to go deer
hunting with his Uncle Johnny that day, and I
decided he would not be at the meeting. But just
as we were about to start, he came in.

To begin his talk, Steve shared an analogy about
some people getting ready to fish but never actually
going fishing. "I love to fish and catch fish, so I
can't imagine anybody just talking about fishing
but never going fishing. However, I recently saw

an illustration which indicated some people are that way.

"Suppose there was a group of men, with enough money to do what they wanted, who decided to start a fishing club. They located a big lake well stocked with fish, built a nice club house, boat pier and covered stalls to keep their nice bass boats. They bought all the latest equipment for fishing. Each boat was equipped with fine reels, rods and every assortment of tackle and lures. Each week they held meetings to discuss fishing techniques. They brought in champion bass fishermen to instruct them on how to catch bass.

"One day a member of the club was talking to a local commercial fisherman about some of the well-known fishermen who gave them instructions. 'I sure would like to hear one of those experts,' he said. The club member responded with an invitation and he attended the next two meetings.

"After the two visits the club member couldn't resist asking the commercial fisherman what he thought about his fishing club. The old fisherman, in an apologetic voice replied, 'I enjoyed your meetings and the fellowship of your members very much, but I don't see how you can call yourself fishermen.'

"'Of course we're fishermen,' said the member. 'Not only do we have the latest in equipment, but we also have a staff who does everything that is needed to help us be knowledgeable in every phase of fishing. Why, we have hired a minister of fishing to look after our boats and an assistant minister to keep up our tackle, plus two secretaries to let us know about meetings and keep our minutes, so how can you say we are not fishermen?'

"The old fisherman patiently responded, 'I know you have all those things, but to call yourself a fisherman, you must go fishing and catch fish. I'm a fisherman; I catch fish. You only talk about fishing. There is a difference.'"

Steve then asked the eight inmates who came to the little prison chapel, "Is this a church of fishers of men? This life is to prepare us for the next life. That preparation can be made wherever a man may be. How many people are in this place? One hundred and twenty-four. Since there are only eight in this meeting, that means you have a lot of fellow inmates to tell about Jesus."

Steve shared his personal testimony that night and concluded with the challenge for everyone to become active fishers of men.

I knew when Steve finished, another fisherman had joined the fleet, as I witnessed the power of the Holy Spirit in his message. That was the first time I heard him share after he called us a few weeks before and told of his rededication to the Lord, which he later termed as salvation. The old Steve would not have driven the forty miles to Camden and returned to Selma that night without having caught "fishing fever" which only comes from the Master's commission.

After that night, I was not surprised when another telephone call came from Steve a few months later, announcing his call to preach the Gospel.

31

God in the Little Things

Life is filled with little, everyday events that add together to make the whole. My faith has grown as I have depended upon God's guidance and help to meet daily needs. I've been further strengthened by the testimony of other believers about the Lord's care for them. Following are some little things that are really big things as we see the hand of the Lord in our daily lives.

God Provided Gas Money

In October of 1983, Rachel and I were helping conduct a Lay-Led Revival at the Farmstead Baptist Church in Jasper, Alabama, and we were staying with the pastor and his wife, the Rev. Billy and Tilda Wooten.

While discussing the reality of God through experiences in our lives, Brother Wooten related a story of "God in action" in his early ministry. "I had started doing a little lay speaking while I was employed as a USPS carrier. One day I left home without any expense money and was 100 miles from Birmingham and about out of gas. Not knowing anyone in town, I wondered what I should do. Then I thought about the Lord and His promise of supplying all our needs, so I prayed for gas money to get back home. Almost immediately the name of the town's postmaster came to mind. In the early days of the USPS, post office employees sometimes resented the new kid on the block, and although they were bound by law to give us addresses, I could tell that their hearts were not always in it. My pride was crushed, but I thought a personal loan would be my only hope.

"As I reluctantly walked to the counter to make my request to the postmaster, a man who worked in the office, whom I had previously chatted with briefly, came to the front. "I hear you started preaching now," he said. "I don't go to church much myself, but I want to give you this five dollars to help you along." Gas was only thirty-five cents a gallon in those days, so I had enough money left to buy a coke and hamburger. I drove back to Birmingham joyfully, knowing that God does provide all our needs when we trust Him," concluded Brother Wooten.

Perhaps we grow most when we learn to pray for the little things and see God answering our prayer when we do not ask amiss. Being a country boy, I have never felt really comfortable driving in heavy traffic, especially entering the busy interstate exchanges. "Lord, create a hole for me so I can get in," is my prayer. He always does. If the Lord knows the very number of hairs on our head, He surely has time to hear both our large and small requests.

Mrs. Dale Gaston, a member of Rachel's Sunday school class in 1982, gave her a counted cross-stitch plaque which sums up God's concern for the little things:

If a Care is too small to be turned into a Prayer,
It is too small to be made into a Burden

Fixing the Tractor Tire

I recall another small instance that happened years ago when Steve was a teenager. It was Saturday, the only day we had to work on the farm that we had purchased while we lived in Perry County. Most of the land had been leased to MacMillan Bloedel Inc. for growing timber, with the exception of a few acres we had reserved for planting wildlife plots. Hunting season would open soon, so we were trying to get the land ready for planting food plots in our limited time. But when we got to the farm, one of the tractor tires was flat, and I had my doubts that we could find a repair shop open to fix it.

Somewhat discouraged about our circumstances, I said to Steve, "Let's pray that we find someone who can fix the tire."

"God's not interested in a little thing like this," was his quick reply. I assured him that He was interested in the little things. We had our prayer, found a place to fix the tire and were back at our work in a few hours.

As I record this instance in September of 1988, I am sure that Steve would be the first to tell anyone that God does indeed have an interest in everything that happens in our life. Otherwise he would not have listened to the prodding of the Holy Spirit to accept salvation and later to commit himself to God's calling for the ministry.

Lord, Open the Gate

In February of 1988, I decided to plant blueberries and muscadines on land where some timber had recently been harvested near our house. I made arrangements with Bobby Wells, a MacMillan Bloedel forester, to cut cedar posts on company land for making the muscadine trellis. The cedar was on a tract used for taking special guests and customers hunting and was blocked by a cable across the access road. Bobby prepared the permit and said he would have the cable down when I got there on Tuesday morning.

I picked up George Kelly at the Work Release Camp at 8:00 A.M., but the cable was still up when we arrived at the tract. "I don't know what happened, but let's have a word of prayer," I said to George. "We can walk in and cut the posts while we wait."

"Lord, give us a safe day as we work, and I pray that you will get the cable down when we cut the posts," I prayed as George, somewhat surprised, bowed his head with me. When we finished our verbal prayer, I silently prayed that God would answer our prayer, not just for my sake, but to show George His reality and that He does care about the little things.

In about two hours we were back at the road only to find that the cable was still up. But as we stepped over the cable a vehicle came to a stop on the highway. I quickly recognized that it was not Bobby, but Sam Lambert, who looks after the company's cooperative hunting.

"You are right on time, not a minute early or a minute late," I said as Sam came to a stop. I explained to Sam that Bobby had given me the cutting permit but somehow had failed to open the cable. As Sam drove away after unlocking the cable, I praised the Lord for hearing our prayer.

"God's timing is always perfect," I said to George. "If we had gotten to the gate a little sooner or later we would have gone to look for Bobby and missed Sam. But the Lord had him there just as we arrived. Always remember that God is not our butler to answer our every little whim, but He is interested in little things. His Word says, "We have not because we ask not," so we should pray about everything. When we do, we can see miracles just as we have seen here today."

Lord, Show Me Someone (October 25, 1990)

When I am going to leave the house each day, I usually put a tract in my pocket and silently pray for the Lord to put someone in front of me to give it to. Sometimes I put one in my pocket even if I do not plan to leave the farm. I can never tell when the Lord may send someone to visit who will need it.

Today, Rachel and I went to Furman to cut a load of cedar posts on her brother Johnny's place. We plan to use the posts to enlarge the muscadine vineyard. I put two tracts in my pocket and said my prayer. I saw some people as we stopped to get gas, but I didn't feel led to talk about a tract. We cut the posts and started home, then made a brief stop at Arnold's store in Furman for a coke.

I was about to get back into the truck when a car pulled up behind and a man motioned for me to come to his window. He had a Disabled Veteran sticker on his car and I noticed a cane inside. He said he was from Montgomery and was seeking directions to Selma. Since he was obviously unfamiliar with the area, I decided the best way for him would be the state highway through Carlowville and gave him directions to it. His first turn would be a few miles in the same direction I was going. He quickly drove away.

As I followed him, I was impressed that I should give him a tract. I felt that I would be unable to do this unless he stopped because I couldn't drive very fast with the load of posts. He wasn't driving fast but was soon out of sight. When I rounded a curve, I saw he had turned on a county road that led to Snow Hill Institute. I blew my horn and motioned for him to follow me to the state highway.

We both stopped when we reached the intersection. I introduced myself and said, "This way is a little further, but I was afraid you would get lost on the back roads. This highway will dead-end into Highway 41, which will lead you into Selma." I knew I didn't have much time. "How do you stand with the Lord?" I asked.

His answer was uncertain. "Let me give you something that will give you the road map to eternal life. There is a way to eternal life just as there is a way to Selma; but if we miss this road map, we miss it all. I had a heart attack over fifteen years ago and heard the music of heaven. That experience changed my priorities of life," I said as I handed him the Eternal Life tract. "I don't think it was an accident that we got together. I hope to see you again."

"Thank you for talking to me," he said sincerely as he drove away.

As I got back into the truck, I thought of another instance that had happened at that same intersection almost a year ago. The circumstances were almost the same, only this time I had a work release man with me. A man from Centerville had spilled a pickup load of very valuable paneling lumber when he made the turn into Highway 28. We stopped and helped flag traffic and reload the lumber.

When we finished, I asked him if he was a Christian. "No, I am not," he said without hesitation.

"Have you ever thought about becoming a Christian?" I asked.

"I can't say that I have," he replied.

"The Bible says that the Spirit which brings salvation appears to all men. It could be that you lost this load of lumber just so the Lord would let me share His reality with you. Maybe He is trying to get your attention. If you have trouble believing that God is real, let me share a couple of times when He has been real to me," I said.

When I had finished, I gave him a tract explaining that it would show him how to become a Christian. I asked if I could have prayer with him. He agreed. I prayed that the Lord would be real to him and meet his needs.

Did he listen just because we helped him get his lumber out of the highway? I don't know. I do know God loves him and all of His creation. He also promises that His word will not return unto Him void but accomplish His purpose.

Today, when Rachel and I got back to Camden, we stopped for a hamburger. I gave the second tract to the waitress. Today was a good day.

Go in the Old Car

In early June of 1986, I had an appointment in Montgomery with Neil Letson of the Alabama Forestry Commission to set up the State FFA Forestry Judging contest. I usually drove our old car, which had over 100,000 miles on it, to work; but I always used our new car for out-of-town trips.

On the appointed morning while I was getting ready to go, an inner voice said, "Go in the old car." It was a rather long trip, almost a hundred miles, and I thought of the possibility of a breakdown; but the thought persisted, "Go in the old blue car." So without comment, I told Rachel that I was taking the old blue car.

The trip was uneventful until I got back to Camden that afternoon so I pondered the meaning of the message. I had even thought that I might have an accident and the new car would not be damaged. I stopped in Camden at a farm supply store and discovered they were having a going-out-of-business sale. All their farm chemicals were being sold at cost, so I purchased several gallons of various herbicides and insecticides, including five gallons of malathion. After the car trunk was filled, two gallons of the malathion were loaded on the floor of the back seat.

When I arrived home, one of the jugs in the back seat had tilted over and a loose cap had allowed half its contents to spill into the floor. I dipped out what I could and tried to dilute the the remainder with a water hose, but the car was ruined. I found out that it's almost impossible to remove concentrate malathion odor from an enclosed place, especially a carpet floor.

We tried several suggested remedies, but none worked. We finally had the carpet removed and replaced, which helped, but we never entirely got rid of the odor.

The car wasn't worth a lot, so other than the frustration and effort to clean it up, it was no big loss. It would have been a lot different with the new car. I'm glad that God expresses His reality in directing our pathways.

32

Light in Total Darkness

...I am the light of the world: he that followeth me shall not walk in darkness... (John 8:12).

Monday night was stormy and rainy. Tornadoes had been sighted in Southwest Alabama. Wilcox County was still in the "watch" area as I went to the Work Release Center for our regular Monday night Bible study. It was my night to lead the discussion and I had chosen the eleventh chapter of Matthew for the text.

We finished the song service led by Peyton Burford. A prisoner who had been released several months before shared his testimony of how God had just given him a job after a waiting period.

I was giving the background of John the Baptist and preparing to talk about his doubts while in prison, when the storm knocked out the lights. There was total darkness in the hallway room where we were holding the service and throughout the complex which houses over 100 prisoners, many doing life sentences.

For a moment, I felt a little of the fear I had several years before when I went to the prison for the first time.

We usually have eight to ten men attend the services, sometimes more when we have a special program. They were seated on benches along the walls. In the total darkness, I could see no one; but I could hear others, who didn't attend the service, passing through the room.

Although I felt a little uneasy, I remembered Paul and Silas' experience in the Philippian jail and their call to the jailer after the lights went out. I asked the men to remain in their seats. We had prayer and continued the service in the pitch dark.

God blessed us with His presence and we concluded the service about twenty minutes later with the "great invitation."

"Come unto me all ye that labor and are heavy laden, and I will give you rest. Take my yoke upon you, and learn of me; for I am meek and lowly in heart: and ye shall find rest unto your souls. For my yoke is easy, and my burden is light" (Matt. 11:28-30).

Jesus is indeed the light of the world as He blessed all of us on a night that was dark on the outside but shining in our hearts. The lights came back on just as we concluded the service.

33

We Shall See God
(Job 19:26)

January 30, 1986

Two days ago a catastrophic explosion blew apart the space shuttle "Challenger," sending seven astronauts to a fiery death eight miles out from the Kennedy Space Center. A school teacher, Sharon Christa McAuliffe from New Hampshire, was one of those aboard.

One minute they were alive and happy as they waved good-by to their families and friends while boarding the ship. Approximately seventy-five seconds after lift-off, they were in eternity.

Our news media has spent hours reporting the tragedy with many side stories about their lives; but I haven't seen anything about their religious belief. I can only hope that each knew Jesus and is now in heaven.

The newspaper before me carries a picture of their smiling faces when they were alive. There were no bodily remains to bury, but Jesus said we would be given a new body when He comes again. Job said long before Jesus came: "For I know that my redeemer liveth, and that he shall stand at the latter day upon the earth: and though after my skin worms destroy this body, yet in my flesh shall I see God" (Job 19:25-26).

I hope that each of the seven could have said the same as Job.

34

Rejection From a Friend

"I was talking with mother last night and she said your old friend, John, (not his real name) has had major surgery," related Rachel as we drank our second cup of coffee following breakfast.

Except for an occasional visit, John and I hadn't seen much of each other in recent years, but we had once been very close, spending time together. "I need to see him as soon as I can," I said.

John seemed glad to see me but was visibly upset about the turn of events with his health. "I always thought that something like this happened to other people, never me," he said. In a few minutes we were alone, but just as I was about to ask John about his eternal salvation, a nurse came to take him for an X-ray. I asked her to give me a couple of minutes for prayer and she agreed, leaving the room. I asked John if he was all right with the Lord. He replied, "I think so," but there was no assurance in his voice.

"Has there ever been a time when you asked Christ to forgive your sins and come into your life and save you?" I could see that John didn't want to talk about it, as he quickly responded that the nurse was waiting. I had a short prayer and beckoned the nurse to return, knowing that I would want to come back another time.

A week later I was at the hospital again. John didn't seem so glad to see me this time. We reminisced about some of our fishing trips and John seemed excited as we talked. But when I said, "As your friend, I want you to be sure of your salvation."

He replied,"You and I don't believe alike."

"It's not what I say but what the Bible says that counts. May I read you what the Bible says about salvation?" He reluctantly agreed, but said for me to make it short.

John had the reputation of being a fine moral man. In all my years of knowing him, I can't recall anyone ever saying an unkind word about him. There are an untold number of people who can remember good deeds John has done for them, and my name could head the list.

As I quickly tried to get through the plan of salvation, using a few verses of Scripture, I could see that John was not with me and was rejecting my witness. I knew to continue would be useless, so I handed him a tract, "Four Spiritual Laws," and asked him if he would read it. He said he might glance at it.

"John, as my friend, will you read it?" I asked.

He gave me no assurance, saying only, "I have lots of friends."

Needless to say I left the room with a heavy heart. My thought was, "Why was I not a more positive witness years ago?"

The day following my visit with John began on a low key. I decided to build a wooden fence across the creek drain which flows from the main fish pond to the river. I planned to leave two openings the width of conibear traps for catching river otters which come into the pond to eat the catfish during the winter months. The narrow openings could also be used to catch any fish which might go through the drain pipe during harvesting operations.

I was half finished with the job when I saw a three-wheeler moving through the woods. Thinking it was a hunter scouting for deer, I caught up with him as he went into a bend in the creek. As we introduced ourselves, he turned out to be the county game warden.

I remembered that his parents had visited our church while they were visiting him, but he had not come. When we had finished our discussion about hunting, I mentioned their visit. "I have to work three Sundays out of each month and I go home on the other Sunday, but they visited the Camden Baptist Church while they were here," he said.

The young man further responded that he was a Christian, but as we talked he told me about his six-year-old daughter and his divorced wife. For a long time we talked about what God could do in our lives in spite of our discouragements and disappointments, if we would just trust Him. Before we parted, we had prayer and asked God to guide our lives in the direction that only He could see. Since his former wife had remarried , I asked God to give him someone else, if it would be His will.

I felt a little better as I went back to building the fence after having the chance to encourage the young warden. I finished the project and went home for lunch and was about to relax with the morning paper when a service truck entered the yard. I was impressed to go talk with the driver about his relationship with the Lord.

Almost twenty years before he had delivered some material when we were building our house. We hadn't talked since, but we remembered each other. I knew he would need to leave soon, so I asked him if he knew the Lord. "I'm not a Christian, if that is what you mean," he said. When I asked if he had thought about the Lord lately, he said "No."

"Do you ever go to church?" I asked.

"Occasionally I go with my wife. I once went regular before we moved to Wilcox county, but I don't go much now," he added.

"You have made the first step toward becoming a Christian," I said.

He looked surprised as he said, "How is that?"

"You have admitted that you are not a Christian. No one can be saved until he recognizes his lostness, and you have done that," I explained.

As he made out the delivery bill, I told him I had a tract I wanted to give him, which he readily accepted and then thanked me for taking the time to talk with him. I promised I would be praying for him as he went on his way. Again, the Lord was easing my hurt for the John's rejection as I felt good about the witness just concluded.

As I stepped inside the house, the phone was ringing. It was the owner of a catfish hatchery and his truck was on the way to deliver me a new batch of fingerlings. When he arrived, the driver attached a chute from the truck tanks and extended it over the lake, and the fish were soon swimming in their new environment. Almost as quickly, I was telling the third man the Lord had sent to me that day about His saving power.

"It's kind of odd, but Mr. Miller's nephew has been telling me about the Lord and how I should go to church, and now you are talking to me like this," said the driver.

"That's the power of the Lord, because He loves you and wants to save you. Since you know you haven't come to Him and accepted Christ as you personal Savior yet, He wants you to do that now," I said as I gave him an invitation after an explanation of what it is to accept Jesus. Although he was visibly touched, he was not yet willing to give up the things of this world and make Jesus Lord. I gave him a tract as he thanked me for talking with him.

I may not know the results of the day until I am in eternity, but I do know my Savior is sufficient to meet all my needs as He eased some of the hurt of John's rejection by giving me the chance to share His love that day.

On Sunday I shared John's rejection with two members of my Sunday School class. One was David Crawford, a young man who is just beginning to pray in public. "I don't know the man, but why don't we pray that the Lord will save him?" he requested. I asked David to lead that prayer, and I have never heard a sweeter, more sincere prayer as he poured out his request to the Lord. I don't believe God will turn down that request.

35

Where Are the Nine?

On a fifth Sunday night community church service in 1986, our pastor, Tommy Davis, reviewed the town's ministry for itinerants and told of the program to give them food and gas. Although it is not expected, Brother Tommy said only one had ever come back to say thank you.

The pastor's report reminded me of a time when Rachel and I had picked up a young man near Chattanooga, Tennessee. His name was Mark and he was carrying a large Bible. Mark was trying to get from a mid-western state to a community in North Florida, or maybe it was South Alabama, where he planned to get married.

Mark was a rather quiet person, but he talked freely about his belief in the Lord. However, he related that he was having trouble understanding the Trinity. He had even been told that the Trinity did not exist. I told Mark that I too had had my difficulties trying to understand the Trinity, but after much prayer, God had given me peace about the subject.

I said to Mark, "There are some things we will never understand. If we knew everything, we would be equal to God. God is not flesh and blood but a spirit. He lived in Jesus as God and He lives in our hearts, when we accept Jesus, as the Holy Spirit. The Trinity is the Father and the Son and the Holy Spirit."

I don't remember all we talked about, but I recall Mark saying before we reached Birmingham, "I prayed that God would send someone to talk with me."

Along the way, we discovered Mark hadn't eaten in two days, so we stopped and ate a hot meal. When we were about to part in Birmingham, I told Mark I wanted to give him $20.00 for a wedding present. I thought this would help him reach his destination. Rachel confided later that she saw a tear in his eye as we said good-by.

A few weeks later a wedding invitation came in the mail from Mark and his future bride. It was his way of saying "thank you." When I think of Mark's humbleness and thankfulness, I remember my own failure to thank God enough for the gift of His Son Jesus and eternal life. Paul wrote in his letter to the Ephesians that we were strangers without hope and without God in the world until we were made near by the blood of Christ. I am thankful that because of His love, I am no longer a stranger—I belong to the household of God!

36

God Saved the Brochure
for Keith

During the later years of my industrial employment, one project was to update a "welcome"
brochure for the company. It was to include a
historical narrative and an explanation of all major
phases of the facilities and their operation through
color photographs and captions. For months I had
been collecting slides and filing material for the
brochure. I was in the final stages of selecting a
company to write the narratives, make the lay-out
and arrange for publication when we had a
downturn in the industry and an austerity program
caused the project to be put on hold.

Economic conditions were better about two
years later, and I received authorization to proceed
with the project. Again, I was almost ready to
contract with another company, but it didn't work
out.

I usually prayed about the projects I undertook
and this one was no exception. Many times I had
asked the Lord to guide me to the right company

to do the job. I believe that God is interested and often reveals Himself in all the affairs of life. I caught myself wondering about His answer to this prayer until I had a chance to sit down and talk with Keith Carpenter.

Keith had called one day while I was thinking about my next move to get the brochure published. "A friend of mine told me that you were interested in publishing a brochure. I have started my own company and would like to talk to you about the job," he said.

Keith drove to the mill site and we discussed the proposed brochure in detail. He brought impressive copies of some of his previous work, and I was convinced he could do the job. I don't remember how our discussion of spiritual experiences came up. Perhaps both of us were sensitive to the leadership of the Holy Spirit and were led to share what the Lord was doing in our lives. When I heard of Keith's faith, I felt sure he was the right person for the project.

He shared an experience that had happened to him several years before. "At the time, I was struggling financially. My wife and I were in church one Sunday night. They were about to take up the collection and all I had was ten dollars, which was going to be my lunch money for the next week. The Lord impressed me to give the ten dollars. I explained to the Lord that was to be my lunch money; but there was the unmistakable urging of the Spirit to give the ten dollars. So I placed the money in the plate when it passed by.

"The next morning as I was about to leave for

work, I was impressed to get a bumper sticker advertising a local radio station which had been lying on the mantel for days. I quickly wiped the dew off the bumper and pasted it on my car and took off. I hadn't gone far when another driver waved for me to stop. He informed me I was their bumper sticker winner for the day and I had just won a prize—a twenty-dollar bill. It was one of my early lessons that God will meet my needs if I trust Him," said Keith.

Keith confided that his finances had been tight since leaving his previous job. "After starting the new company, I was concerned about how I was going to keep up the payments on my house. I did my share of worrying until finally I said, 'Lord, if you want me to give up the house and move back into a rental apartment, that's what I'll do. You just guide me into whatever direction I need to go.' After I prayed that prayer, the Lord began to open doors, and I have been able to keep the house."

Keith was especially gifted in art. He went back home and, using the outline I had given him, he put together an artistic proposal for the brochure. His quote for the finished project was within the budget. "If I get this job from a large company like yours, it will open the door to other firms who need similar products," said Keith. We gave Keith the contract and his work was everything we hoped for and expected.

Rachel and I had the pleasure of sharing more of our Christian experiences with the Carpenters as we visited and worked together during the production of the brochure. The whole experience reaffirms the reality of God in all our affairs of life. Looking back, where it is sometimes easier to see the working of God, I believe that the Lord did save the brochure for a young man who was trusting Him to meet his needs.

But time has revealed much more of Keith's story. A couple of years after I retired, I called Keith and told him I was writing this book and had included this chapter. "I've started doing 'Chalk Talks for the Lord' since I last saw you," he explained excitedly.

Keith had mentioned that possibility when I had commented about his artistic ability while he was working with the brochure. "I saw a man do a chalk talk when I was a young boy and I have never forgotten the spiritual message he brought through the medium of art. I have been thinking about putting something together and doing that someday," Keith had said.

I talked to my pastor and he invited Keith to come to Camden in July of 1991 for a presentation to our congregation. Keith did two drawings, the first titled "Creation," and the second, "God Is Eternal." Keith preceded the drawings with his personal testimony, then directed all eyes to his easel by having the lights turned off in the auditorium. "When the room is darkened, a person becomes alone with God. He doesn't think about his pew neighbor as he is led by the power of the Holy Spirit through the tape message and the drawing," Keith explained while discussing his procedure. Our church fellowship, from our youth to senior adults, still talk about the spiritual message in Keith's presentation.

In May of 1992, Keith and his daughter, Kerri, along with their new family member, Cindy Lu, joined us for a four-day, Lay-Led Revival at New Hope Baptist Church in Pell City, Alabama, where Rev. Tommy Turner has pastored for seventeen years. The Carpenters led the service on Saturday night. James Kennedy, a Lay Team member and staff writer for the Birmingham News, was present. The following is quoted from a newspaper article James wrote.

"Soft gospel music—flavored with Bible verses, hymns and narration—played as the artist swiftly drew a pastoral scene on a large canvas...First came distant mountains, then green, rolling hills, trees, a small country church and cemetery, a road, splashes of colorful spring flowers.

"As the artist stepped away from the canvas, the taped voice said, 'Things which are seen are temporal, and things which are not seen are eternal.'

"He adjusted some lights. A broad cross, jutting from the church to an opening in the sky, slowly appeared on the canvas as if by magic, at first pale, then a brilliant gold. The church's stained-glass windows glowed as if lit from inside, as the scene was bathed in different shades of reds, oranges, yellows and pinks.

"People figures from the church marched up the cross toward the equally brilliant opening in the sky, a gateway to a heavenly city. The tape played, 'Precious Lord Take My Hand'...Keith Carpenter, the artist, eased back into a front-row pew of the darkened church, and for several minutes the only sounds were those from subdued crying."

It was a time for lost people to come to Jesus. It was a time for re-dedication of Christians to evangelism as they observed the figures of the dead, walking the cross of Christ to heaven, because of the witness of a faithful grandmother in the rural church community which Keith had just portrayed. It was also a time to think again of our own walk to that heavenly city some day. Such was the prevailing spirit in the subdued quietness of New Hope Baptist Church that Saturday night.

Keith's daughter, Kerri, who recently joined the team, had begun the service with a ventriloquistic comedy act based on Christian principles. Only fourteen, she had performed like a professional as she led "Cindy Lu" through her dialog.

Keith and his wife, Sharon, Kerri, and their son Chris, live in Fulton, Mississippi. The Carpenters are another example of what the Lord can do with lay people when they are willing to use their gifts for the building of His kingdom.

37

Tribute to Daddy

(Recorded December 3, 1986)

For thirty-five years, Thanksgiving was a special day for my daddy and his family. It was our annual reunion time, a tradition which began after my sister, two brothers and I were grown and married with our own families. Our mother died in her early forties. Daddy remarried and moved to Paxton, Florida, where he and my brother Bernard went into farming. Daddy's second wife died and he remarried a third time. After a few more years, this wife also died and then he lived alone until Bernard gave up farming and moved from the adjoining farm.

Throughout the thirty-five years, daddy insisted that we all come home for Thanksgiving. Most of the years our visits carried right on into Sunday afternoon. The countryside was full of quail. We had good bird dogs, and Thanksgiving sunrise would find us in the fields following the dogs. The ladies served turkey on Thanksgiving day, but Friday the menu was always quail. It was not unusual for us to kill fifty to a hundred birds. I think we enjoyed the Friday meal best of all.

When our children were born and began to grow up, they joined the hunts. Then deer began to populate the country and we changed our hunts for the bucks.

But everything has an end and our reunion was no exception. We observed our last Thanksgiving at the peaceful farm house in the woods in 1985. My sister Jeanette got daddy a retirement apartment in Loxley in the complex where one of his brothers lived. The complex was only three miles from Rosinton, where he was raised. It was also near Jeanette's home, so she could check on his needs regularly.

We planned to continue the tradition of holding the family reunion at Thanksgiving. Since I was the oldest, the 1986 get-together would be at my house. We made plans for daddy to come up with Jeanette and her family and then stay an extra week. Trapping season had just come in, so I thought he and I would do a little trapping around the pond.

Sunday before Thanksgiving, I felt the urge to call him. He told me about his recent trip back to his old place in Florida and a visit to Bernard's for a week. We talked about Thanksgiving and this first one away from his farm. We talked about the trapping we would do. We talked for several minutes. At our conclusion, I said, "I'll see you."

Two days later, daddy was about to make his morning walk when the Lord called him. We buried him on Thanksgiving eve beside my mother in the Rosinton Road Cemetery. We cancelled our Thanksgiving get-together and agreed that from that point on we would spend the holiday with our own family and set aside another day for the reunion.

My daddy was eighty-three years old and had enjoyed good health all his life. During his stays with me, he always commented shortly after arrival, "Boy, I've got to have a job." I always had plenty.

Back home on Thanksgiving Day, I walked around the farm. Everywhere were memories of daddy's semiannual visits and the jobs he had done: The 400 young pecan tree trunks he had painted the previous spring (to keep out the borers) glistened in the sun; the utility buildings he had helped construct; the brick he cleaned from an old chimney; the woods where he cleared the under-brush near the house; and the places he trapped the coons and otters around the catfish ponds. On and on the list went. It was time to shed some tears, which I hadn't done before, as I fully realized the loss of a loved one.

My daddy didn't accumulate much of this world's goods, but each place I looked, I saw those reminders of his love to me. The same exists for my brothers and sister and many others he came in contact with. Like us, he was not perfect; but his influence will long live because he gave his greatest virtue to all—his love.

Typical is an incident that happened when I was in the seventh grade at Rosinton. Our junior high basketball team was going to Bay Minette to play in an all day county tournament. My first cousin and fellow team member, Teddy Cooper, said, "Why don't you ask your daddy for some money. We will be there all day."

Money came hard at our house, so I seldom asked for anything extra. Daddy's wage for a day's work was probably not more than a dollar. Nevertheless, at Teddy's urging, I asked, expecting maybe a dime which would buy a Coke and piece of candy.

I'll never forget what he gave to me. "You'll be there all day, take this dollar."

It was fitting that Bernard, who has been called to preach, be led of the Lord to read the thirteenth chapter of First Corinthians as a final tribute to daddy during his funeral.

38

When a Blue Light Comes On

(Recorded February 12, 1989)

"Daddy, the annual boat show is in Birmingham this weekend, so why don't you come up and we will see the boats on Saturday," said my son Steve as he called from his home in Coosa County on Thursday night.

For a long time Steve had encouraged me to buy a bass boat. His persuasion continued as he said, "You are retired now, and you ought to get a boat that you can handle easily without having to drag that old "John boat" up and down the bank. With a new boat, you can fish all over the lake and not be confined to the one place you fish without a motor.

"I just got back from fishing on Lay Lake and caught seven nice bass, and I didn't go until after school was out. If you can get here by three o'clock, we can go fishing and then go to Birmingham on Saturday," he added.

I had thought and prayed about getting a bass boat since retirement. Rachel and I had about decided that we would buy one, so I accepted Steve's invitation and told him I would be there in time to go fishing Friday evening.

Friday morning I checked out a man from the Work Release Camp who had been helping me on the farm. I thought the morning would give us ample time to prune Mrs. Virginia Watts' home orchard. Virginia is one of our faithful church members who had torn ligaments in her knee when she fell while working in the orchard and I had promised to finish the job for her. The pruning took a little longer than I expected. I didn't get away from home until almost one o'clock, but there would still be time to get to Steve's by three o'clock. Little did I realize the delay that was to come.

I set the speed control and all went well until I got near Selma; then I began to get involved with traffic which continued until I got off the bypass and onto the state highway leading to Highway 14. I suppose it was the sudden release of the slow traffic, then almost none at all, that made me speed up. Almost immediately I realized I was going too fast and quickly slowed down. I noticed a car coming about a mile down the road, but I didn't recognize it as a highway patrol car until it drew closer and then the blue light began to flash.

I knew I had had it, and I knew I was guilty. The young trooper said I was speeding and he would have to give me a citation as he invited me into the front seat of his car. I was perplexed. This would be my first citation in forty years of driving.

After giving him the necessary information, I said, "I know I'm guilty, and I guess I'll have to pay a fine. I've been guilty of greater things than traffic violations, but I am thankful that someone else paid my fine for that."

"Is that right?" said the trooper in a quizzical voice.

"Yes, Jesus Christ paid my fine for all my sins against God. When I accepted Him, He assured me of eternal life in heaven when I die," I explained. "The Bible says that everyone has sinned but in heaven there will be no sin. As sinners we cannot go there unless we are somehow cleaned up. The cleaning process takes place when we accept Jesus whose shed blood on the cross washes away our sin. He paid our fine." I saw the young trooper was interested, so I continued.

"Let me give you an illustration. Suppose you went to the Alabama River and got in a boat and started to paddle it across. You didn't know the plug was out until you were half way across and the boat was about to sink. You can't swim so it looks like you will drown. But just before the boat goes under, another boat comes down the river, sees your plight, and pulls you out. I literally had that happen to me years ago when a friend and I were fishing on the Warrior River. I saw a boat much faster than mine coming from up river. When it didn't pass, I looked back to see three heads bobbing in the water. Two of the men were almost drowned by the time I got back to them. I guess in a way I was their earthly savior, just as the person who pulled you out would be. It's the same way with us getting out of this "sea of life." We must have a savior, and that Savior is Jesus Christ.

"If you have trouble believing there is life after this life, let me share an experience I had fourteen years ago," I said.

Before he could respond, his radio came on and he had to communicate with his dispatcher. Then he turned back to me and inquired, "You were telling me about an experience you had?"

As I began to share the near-death experience when I had the heart attack in 1974, I could tell that the Holy Spirit was dealing with the young trooper. I told him of the beautiful music I heard, of being outside my body, of knowing the Lord had let me hear a little of the sound of heaven that night because I had accepted Jesus as a young man.

"Here, let me give you something that explains what a man must do to have eternal life," I said as I reached in my shirt pocket and gave him the tract, "Four Spiritual Laws." "That's the plan of salvation. Read it and it will explain what a person must do to be saved. But before I go, let me have prayer with you.

"Lord, I broke man's law and I will have to pay a fine; but I thank you that you paid my biggest fine a long time ago, as well as the fine for every person who desires eternal life. I pray now that you will bless this trooper. Keep him safe in his job and Lord, meet his needs, whatever they may be."

As we shook hands, he said, "Thank you for the literature."

By this time a light rain had begun to fall. I could see the trooper's car in my rear view mirror a long way as I drove down the straight highway. His lights were still on and the car had not moved when I finally reached a curve and could see him no more. I believe he read the tract through before he moved.

I may not know the results of this witness until I am with the Lord. What I do know is that God gave me an opportunity to share His good news during an unpleasant circumstance. Life is full of unpleasant circumstances, but God can use each event to His glory if we will be sensitive to the leadership of the Holy Spirit. Paul and Silas, who were unjustly thrown into the Phillipian jail, could have asked God "why?" However, they sang praises and the Lord used their faithfulness to save the Phillipian jailer.

I was twenty minutes late getting to Steve's house, but it made no difference because the rain continued throughout the afternoon. Jesus said He would make us fishers of men if we would follow Him.

39

Lord, Give Me Some Fruit

Dr. Henry Lyons III, Director of Family and Deacon Ministries of the Alabama Baptist Convention, had invited me to share my testimony at the 1989 Deacon's Rally in Birmingham and again the following week at a similar meeting in Montgomery. I had already shared in Birmingham, and although it seemed to go well, I wanted the Lord to bless me with something fresh for the Montgomery presentation that would build upon the theme of "Witnessing As We Go."

I had also prayed for new experiences before going to the Birmingham meeting. I had told the group about witnessing to the highway patrolman, mentioned in the previous chapter, and to a boat salesman who sold me a new boat. Although I believe God blesses every testimony of His greatness, I didn't know the results of either witness.

I tried to help God answer my prayer, "Lord if you saved these two men and they let me know about it, then I would have something new and special to share in Montgomery." The boat salesman had said as I was about to drive away with the new boat, "I thank you for your business, but most of all I thank you for your concern for me. I'll read the tract." He had my address, as did the highway patrolman.

I'm slowly learning that I can't tell God how to do things. His Word says, "My ways are not your ways." The days passed and I heard nothing from these two men. But the Lord still heard my prayer and gave me fruit during that week which was far beyond my expectations.

It started Monday night at the Wilcox County jail during the weekly prison ministry conducted by Peyton Burford, Jimmy Simpkins and myself. I talked to about a dozen men in the main cell block. I don't remember all that I shared, but I do remember telling them about the first man I ever led to the Lord fourteen years before in that same cell. I recounted that I had talked with the man each Monday night for six weeks. I told them how the Lord had dealt with him as well as myself each week.

I explained, "God had to first show me that the man in the cell was no different in His eyes than myself. Until that time, I had always felt that if a man got put into jail, he got what he had coming to him. God had to again make me aware of His grace through Jesus Christ's shed blood that brought me salvation.

"Just because that man was in jail, as you are, made him no different from anyone else in the eyes of God. Every person is in a type of jail until he is set free by Jesus. Jesus said that you shall know the truth and the truth shall make you free. When we realize we need a Savior because we are sinful people and are willing to repent of those sins and put our trust in Jesus, then we can be saved."

I told the men how the Lord gave me a love and a burden for the man as the weeks went by. "On the last night he would be in Camden, before being transferred to a State Prison, he knelt with me and asked Jesus to forgive him for his sins," I said as I pointed out the place we were fourteen years ago.

Again, I don't remember all that was said that night, but I do remember the power of the Holy Spirit as I shared. When I gave the invitation, nine men knelt on the floor and asked Jesus for salvation.

I still believed God was going to save the patrolman and the boat salesman. I fully expected to hear something each day.

I had made plans with Mr. Groom to take the boat I had bought the week before on its maiden fishing trip on Thursday. I stopped at one of our local bait shops for gas and minnows. The young man who helped service the boat was a person I had talked to about Jesus over a year ago. As we talked about church attendance, I noticed another young man who was pumping gas into my pickup. Turning my attention to the teenager, I asked him if he knew the Lord. He acknowledged that he didn't know the Savior.

"Here, let me give you something that will show you how you can know Him," I said as I took an Eternal Life tract from my shirt pocket. He readily accepted it and I was soon on my way to meet Mr. Groom at the boat ramp.

Friday morning Rachel and I were enjoying a second cup of coffee as we completed our daily devotional reading when a knock came at the door. It was a catfish feed salesman and we invited him to join us at the breakfast table.

We completed our business about the feed and then began a casual conversation. He mentioned a job with another company until he had open heart surgery three years ago.

"You and I have something in common," I said. "I haven't had surgery, but I did have a heart attack fourteen years ago. God gave me an unusual experience while my son was driving me to the hospital. I actually felt my spirit leave my body and heard the music of heaven," I said as I explained the details of the attack. "Did you have such an experience during your sickness and operation?" I asked.

"No." he replied.

"I am not sure why the Lord gave me that experience, unless He wanted me to share it. I know it goes back to the time I asked the Lord for salvation when I was on a burning ship in a storm. When I had the heart attack, I was on my way to heaven because I had trusted in Jesus as my Savior. Have you had that experience? Do you know that if you had died during your heart surgery you would have gone to heaven?"

"No, I don't," he replied as he slowly shook his head.

"Would you like to know?" I asked.

Again, without hesitation, he said, "Sure would." So I took the Bible and explained some key verses that relate to God's plan of salvation, concluding with Romans 10:9,10 and 13. "If you believe that Jesus did die for your sins, that He arose again, and you are willing to repent of your sins and ask Him to save you, He will, as we have just read. Would you like to do that right now?" I asked.

He said yes to Jesus and became my brother in Christ. As he left my house that morning his parting words were, "Thank you. You are the first man who has ever taken time to explain the Word of God the way you have."

At four o'clock that afternoon I picked up Fred Sheffield, a fellow deacon, to go to Montgomery for the Deacon's Rally. We stopped at the bait shop for gas. The young man I had given the tract to was manning the pumps. "Did you read that booklet I gave you yesterday?" I asked as he filled the tank.

"I sure did. That was some good reading; and I prayed that prayer, too," he said with a big smile on his face.

That night I shared several other things, but the gist of the presentation was what the Lord had done that week, as I went. God had heard my prayer and let me invite eleven people to know him.

I haven't heard anything from the patrolman or the boat salesman. God has promised that the Word will not return void. I believe I'll see both men in heaven if I never see them again on earth. In the meantime, the Lord will give us the experiences we need to share the good news.

40

Catch Me, Lord

(Recorded October 15, 1983)

It was a beautiful fall day, a perfect day to be outside under a clear blue sky. The gorgeous hickory leaves dominating the hillside across the lake were at their peak in yellow and burnt orange colors.

I was in the process of building an addition onto our equipment shed, and with the aid of two young men, we were making good time. One of the men was named Peter, a senior in high school. The other was Johnny, who now had a full-time job at a local plant. Johnny had been my regular helper during his school years and still came to help me on Saturday when I had a special need.

We finished putting up the last rafter by noon and by midafternoon all the plywood roof decking was in place. I did most of the ground work while the two men nailed the decking. The last job with the decking was to make a trim cut from the ridge to the overhang along the gable end. After they had struck a chalk line, I decided to go onto the roof and make the cut with an electric hand saw. I didn't think either of them were experienced enough with the saw to cut a straight line.

I ascended the ladder and was about to step on the roof when the ladder started slipping sideways. I had the unpleasant dilemma of either falling with the ladder, or trying to somehow reach the roof. My position, although only for an instant, was like having one foot on a dock and the other in a boat that is moving away.

I chose the roof and gave a last-second quick lunge and landed on both knees on the roof. But I couldn't balance on the steep angle and I began to slide the few inches that would carry me to a rough, twelve-foot fall that might have been fatal to a fifty-six-year-old man.

Before I had time to think that I was a goner, I felt Peter's strong hand catch the sleeve of my shirt, but my weight was too great and I was dragging Peter with me. In almost the same instant, Johnny, who was farther up the roof, grabbed Peter and stopped our slide.

The next day at Sunday School, as I related the incident to my Couples Class, God reminded me that He will be with us and will be there to catch us when we are about to fall—if we always ask Him. Not just in our physical falls, but in everything—temptations, financial difficulties, health problems, relationships or whatever. The key is in the asking. As Peter, Johnny and I had eaten our lunch earlier, we had thanked God for a good and safe morning and asked Him to keep us safe that afternoon.

41

Harvesting the Fish

For sixteen years we have been raising channel catfish in a fourteen-acre, horseshoe lake which is overlooked from our house. Usually a harvest is made each year and the fish are sold to a processing plant in Greensboro, Alabama. We lower the level of the water through a drain pipe controlled by a valve and then seine the fish and load them into large aerated tanks and transport by truck to the plant.

This year the price was good so we decided to sell in early May; however when we took a sample fish, it was off flavor, a condition caused by too much algae in the lake. Weekly samples followed, but the condition of the water did not change. Retirement time came at the end of May and still the fish were off flavor. I took another fish to the plant and was told that sometimes the addition of lime to the water would restore the flavor. On Saturday, with my son-in-law Neil's help, we limed the lake.

Throughout the six weeks we had been trying

219

to sell the fish, I had been praying that things would work out before the price went down or the fish took a disease or some other problem happened. I also thought about the $12,000 note I owed for the feed and how that would eat into my retirement savings if we lost the fish for some reason.

It was my time to speak at Wednesday night prayer meeting which the deacons were doing while we were without a pastor. I had been pruning about 200 Christmas trees we have on the farm and was led to speak of the pruning process a tree must have to be shaped for the market. I used this illustration to speak of our own pruning which is nothing more than to learn to trust God rather than our own selves as quoted in John 15: 1-8. But, like so much I know and can quote from the Scriptures, I often fail to apply it to my everyday life. Looking back, I can see that I needed some more pruning in learning patience and waiting on the Lord for the right time to harvest the fish.

After the liming, I carried another sample to the processing plant and this time they were back on flavor. The harvesting day was set and we were blessed with almost 50,000 pounds of fish and the price went up another two cents rather than decline. Needless to say, I felt foolish about any apprehension I had.

The grape vines I have in my orchard must be pruned each year. I am no different.

42

A Good Day

June, 1988

After sixteen years of raising catfish, the stand which houses the control valve for draining and filling the pond rusted away and collapsed just as we were getting ready to sell a crop of fish. I was able to make a temporary wooden stand which allowed us to drain the pond so we could harvest the fish. In addition, the deep water release sleeve pipe also rusted out. Both of these had to be replaced before the next filling of the pond. Both would be difficult and dangerous to do without a crane or some other lifting equipment to which I did not have access.

A local machinist made a new valve stand and had sufficient help to get it up, but the large pipe had to be purchased from a dealer and coated with tar. It weighed almost 500 pounds and was thirty-four inches in diameter, making it very bulky to handle. It was eight feet high and had to be set over the top of the twelve-foot high overflow stand pipe.

With the help of Phillip Huff Jr., we built a platform on piers even with the top of the stand pipe. My plan was to get the pipe from the dam to the platform, stand it on end, and slide it over the pipe. I soon realized this would be impossible by hand. I next decided to build a overhead frame another 10 feet in the air to lift the pipe with a rope and pulley, then lower it over the stand pipe.

From the beginning, both Rachel and I did a lot of praying about this project. I especially prayed for the safety of those I would have helping me.

On the day before I was to get some men from the Work Release Center to help install the pipe, Larry and Phillip Huff were helping me seine catfish fingerlings. After we finished, I decided to get the pipe part of the way to the platform from the dam. We had almost reached a stopping point when a piece of lumber broke loose, and the pipe crashed toward the ground and Larry. Phillip and I both saw that the pipe was about to hit Larry and for a split second were able to hold it long enough to give him time to get out of the way.

Was it luck, or our own strength, or the reality of God answering prayer which prevented us from having someone hurt? I felt the presence of the power of God and His protection.

We repaired the skids leading from the dam to the platform and I got three men from Work Release the next day. I explained what had to be done, the danger involved and gave them the opportunity to withdraw if they wanted. They said,"We can do the job." Before we started, I explained to them my belief in God, that we had a guardian angel to help take care of us until the time Jesus called us home. I had prayer for our safety and the success of the job before we began. In spite of their backgrounds which had led to them doing time in a correctional institution, I could tell that they were touched by the testimony and prayer.

We got the pipe to the platform and in an upright position without too much trouble; then we built the ten-foot frame above it to attach the pulley for lifting the pipe and swinging it over the stand pipe. The beam for holding the pulley was a 2" x 6" board held in place by blocks to keep it from sliding sideways. We could not easily reach the top to nail it but thought the down weight would hold the beam in place.

Three of us stood on the ground and tried to lift the pipe with the rope pulley while the other man attempted to swing it over the standpipe. What we didn't realize was that the top beam was shifting toward one end each time we pulled on the rope. We strained every muscle but still the pipe couldn't be pushed far enough. And then I saw it. The beam had no more than a half an inch of support left before everything would come tumbling down on top of the man on the platform and perhaps those on the ground.

We held our breath while the rope was untied and the beam repositioned from a ladder and nailed. On our next effort we got the pipe in place and had a prayer of thanks for God's care.

Then I went to town and bought the men lunch. As we ate, I shared a tract of how they could become Christians. But I think the real testimony had already been given by the Lord in keeping us safe, as we had asked Him before we began the job.

I may never know the results of the witness that day until I am with the Lord, but one of the men commented as we finished lunch, "This has been a good day."

43

The Lord's Championship Game

Our local high school, Wilcox Academy, made it to the championship game in the state football playoff in 1985. Several of the players attended my church, including Frank McIntosh who would later be a quarterback at Auburn University. I was looking forward to seeing this game as I was flying home from Kansas City on Friday after attending the national FFA Convention where I served on a committee for their Forestry Judging Contest.

I was to change planes in Memphis for a direct flight to Montgomery and then would have plenty of time to drive home before the game. But at boarding time in Memphis, we were told the flight had been cancelled and there would be a five-hour delay.

Disappointed, I walked to the main lobby of the airport to get something to read and a bite to eat. I remembered another time about three years before in the same news stand, when I had bought a book titled, *I'm Not There Yet, But I'm Better Than I Was.*

It was written by a local black woman, Francis Kelly, whom God had given a gifted singing voice.

Francis wrote of her early childhood, singing in night clubs and a husband who took her to a northern city where he gave her a big house, furs and fine cars. Then family problems led to failing health and divorce. When Francis became desperate, God led her to a caring church where she found the Lord. She moved back to Memphis, joined a prayer group, and was miraculously healed. Francis was hired by a local TV station to host a talk show titled "Wake Up Memphis" as the first black newscaster in the city.

When Billy Graham led a revival in Memphis, she gave her testimony and sang a solo. In addition to TV, she got a job with American Airlines, sometimes working at the ticket counter. Throughout the book, she shared many spiritual experiences which were an inspiration to me, and the Lord had led me to use excerpts in witnessing to others. I had tried to meet Francis as I traveled through Memphis, but she was never on duty and I had about forgotten her. As I was checking out of the news stand, I remarked to the cashier that I had once bought a book written by Francis Kelly, a local person.

"She's right across the aisle at the ticket counter," was her reply as she smiled and pointed toward Francis.

I introduced myself to Francis and said I had enjoyed her book. I don't know how long we talked, but it was several minutes as we each shared blessings of the Lord. The Lord kept everyone away during our conversation, as not a single person came for a ticket. It was an inspirational time for me, and I think it was for her, as we shared the goodness of God.

I returned to my waiting area and began a conversation with a man who was on my flight. I shared my meeting with Francis and how she came to know the Lord, plus my own testimony. As I talked, I noticed two other people seemed to be listening, so I spoke loud enough for them to hear. The man seemed to be touched as I shared my belief in Jesus as Savior and my salvation experience on the ship years before.

When we were finally in flight, I was seated by a young black girl who lived in Montgomery. She worked for UPS and had been to Memphis for a training seminar. She was excited about her work and talked about Memphis being the hub for delivering UPS parcels. But Francis Kelly's story provided the lead to get her attention to talk about Jesus and salvation.

It was 11:00 P. M. when I got home. The ball game was long since over and Camden was quiet as I drove through the little town on my way home. But I didn't feel bad about not seeing the championship game. As it turned out, my school team lost; but I felt that I had been in the midst of a conflict that was far more important. Witnessing about the saving power of Jesus is certainly not a game; but it is a conflict with Satan, who doesn't want to see anyone come to Jesus. However, sharing Jesus is the only activity I know of which assures success before we start. Isaiah 55:11 proclaims that God's

Word will not return void but accomplish His purpose. When we share the Word, we are letting others know of the greatest championship of all: "Victory in Jesus!"

44

Witnessing As We Go

December 3, 1988

Only three people showed up for Tuesday night church visitation—Brother Eddie Davidson, Edwina LeCroy and myself. We tried to make three visits in the Miller's Ferry area but found no one home at either stop. But the Lord had already filled my cup that day by allowing me to see four men pray to receive Christ. I didn't have to go visiting because the Lord sent them to me at the farm. Again, I was able to experience the reality of witnessing "as we go."

I don't mean to say that there is not a special place for a church visitation program, but I really believe the greater opportunity is in our everyday activities, if we will only be sensitive to the needs of those Christ puts in front of us. This week it was a logging crew God sent my way.

For several years I had thought about cutting some of the trees bordering the pecan orchards because they keep the sunlight from reaching the pecans. Now that retirement had come , I took the time to negotiate a cutting plan with Jimmy Travis, a local wood dealer, and his logging crew came on Monday.

I had done a lot of praying for the right crew to cut the trees and for their safety while working. The logging contractor who came was a man I had known for years but had lost contact with for a long time. After his crew started to work, he helped me catch some catfish for our annual deacon's supper we were hosting Thursday night, so I had a good chance to visit with him and also talk about his relationship with the Lord. He assured me he was a Christian.

The weather had turned cool and the fish didn't bite very well. I was beginning to think I might have to go buy fish to feed the twenty-seven guests we were having Thursday. On Tuesday at mid-morning I tried to catch the fish again, and my friend joined me to help. This time we had good luck, and by noon I had all I needed.

We were talking to the logging crew as they broke for lunch, and I had gotten in my truck to leave when the Lord reminded me I had prayed the night before asking for a chance to share with them. I got out of the pickup and asked the foreman if it would be all right to share with the men while they finished their lunch. With his permission, I began:

"Fellows, none of us actually owns anything. We just get to use it for a while during our short lifetime. This place, these trees, are really God's, and He is just letting me be His steward. I would be doing the Lord and you an injustice if I let you come out here and work without telling you what He has done for me and what He will do for you, if you surrender to His will.

"Is God real? I expect that every man asks that question at some point in his life. Perhaps you have? Let me tell you about the time Christ first became real to me."

As I related my childhood prayer of asking God to "let the milk cow be in the pen when I get home," I could sense that they were warming to the power of the Holy Spirit as they identified with their own childhood. I related that even though God had revealed himself to me, that experience didn't make me a Christian. There had to be a time of surrender to the lordship of Christ, after I recognized that without forgiveness and acceptance of Jesus, I was destined for hell. I shared my salvation experience and related it to the two thieves who were crucified with Jesus.

"One thief thought only of this world as he suffered until his death; but the other saw himself as getting what he deserved while he saw Jesus as the Son of God. When he confessed his sin and asked Jesus for mercy and a place in heaven, he exercised the faith that we too must do to inherit eternal life."

I reviewed the Scripture verses which point to the plan of salvation and ended with Romans 10:9-10, 13. I asked if anyone in the group had ever confessed their sins and asked Jesus to come into their life and save them. There were several vocal "no's."

"On behalf of the Lord, if you mean business

and truly want to be saved and are willing to make Jesus Lord of your life, He will save you now. Right here. Is there anyone who would like to do this?"

Throughout my sharing, I noticed that there was one black man who seemed reluctant to hear me, so I was surprised when he was the first to say, "Yes, I want to be saved." Three other men joined him.

As we gathered around the pickup truck, hats removed, those four men asked Christ to come into their lives. I told them that the song, "Amazing Grace," has a verse that says "When we've been there ten thousand years, we've just begun." I added that we would have plenty of time to remember our prayer around this pickup truck.

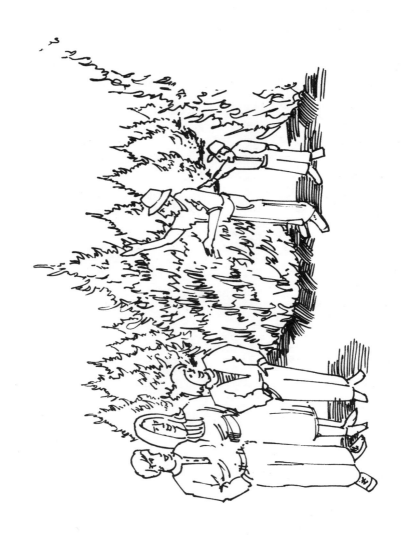

45

Christ and Our Christmas Tree Farm

Somewhere about the time of my retirement from MacMillan Bloedel in May of 1988, I was the speaker for our church's Wednesday night prayer service. The Lord led me to use an analogy of a farm job I had been doing—pruning 250 Christmas trees. Because of past neglect due to insufficient time, I was having to do severe cutting of the branches to get the young trees shaped properly. As I worked in the summer heat, I thought of the words written in the fifteenth chapter of John where Jesus talked about the vine and the branches and how the branches must be pruned so that they will be fruitful.

I have used the story of the vine and the branches for several years in the prison ministry. Each year I cut a vine with a big cluster of grapes and take it to the Jail and Work Release Camp to demonstrate how I must prune my two plants so they will bear fruit. We then talk about how Jesus is the Vine and we are the branches, and how a branch cannot bear fruit of itself. Without Jesus, we can do nothing. Jesus further said that if a man abide not in Him, he is cast forth into the fire as a discarded branch and burned.

I always take extra grapes for the prisoners to enjoy. We close with Christ's promise that if we abide in Him, we shall bear much fruit and we can ask for what we will. God has used this parable to speak to several men who have accepted Jesus during the invitation.

As I spoke to our church congregation that week, I talked about how we as Christians must also be pruned to be fruitful. Sometimes it hurts. We can only ask that God be gentle with us. But just as the Christmas tree must be injured with the blade of the shear before it will become dense and beautiful, we also must be pruned.

The highlight of my talk that night (at least to me) was relating to the group the prayer I had prayed that day. I had prayed, "Lord, don't let these trees just be a Christmas ornament for some family. Make each one special in which you will be glorified on your birthday."

Looking back, I didn't do a very good job of teaching my children the real meaning of Christmas. I told the church I was going to try to do better with my grandchildren.

As I write these words tonight, it has been two summers since I prayed that prayer and asked God to glorify each tree. I don't know how Jesus will answer my prayer, but I believe He will.

About half the trees are ready for the market and are being sold as "pick your own" trees. The

Lord led me to write some thoughts about the trees which I am giving to each purchaser. The following is the Christmas tree "thoughts" which I am giving those who get a tree.

Some Thoughts About Your Christmas Tree

Thank you for purchasing a Pebble Hill Christmas tree. I sincerely hope it adds joy to your family and friends during this special time of the year.

I don't know when the tradition of bringing a green tree into our homes and decorating it with ornaments had its beginning, or what purpose the originator had in mind for that first tree. Perhaps someone wanted to use the analogy to bring new remembrance of what Christ had done for us during His earthly mission.

Maybe the growing tree, as it was cut away from its life in the forest, was to represent the life of Christ which He gave on another tree to redeem mankind for his sins. The thought might have been to highlight the joy of the beginning, the birth of the Savior. Just as the wise men who followed the star and brought gifts, the Christmas tree would be decorated as gifts to the Christ Child. Since the tradition was begun at Christmas, it was no doubt to glorify the the birth of Christ.

As I pruned these trees last year, I asked the Lord to make each tree special to someone at Christmas. I asked that it would be more than just a holiday decoration, that He would be glorified through each tree.

As I thought on the meaning of Christmas, I was reminded by the Lord that I had not always done a good job of teaching my children the real meaning of Christmas. I resolved then that I would try to do better with my grandchildren. When they came home for Christmas, we read the Christmas story from the first and second chapter of the Gospel of Luke and talked about why Christ was born. Then we opened our presents.

Again, I hope this tree will not only contribute joy to you and your family at Christmas, but that it will also serve as a reminder of Christ's mission as written in Matthew 1:21.

46

Fortieth Class Reunion

July 8, 1985

A year ago I was attending an annual meeting of the Alabama Forestry Association at Gulf Shores, Alabama. I had planned to have dinner with a group, but I was a little late getting to the hotel lobby and discovered that they had already left. I looked around for someone else to eat with but saw no one I knew. As I approached my car, thinking about where to eat, I suddenly remembered an old friend and classmate whom I had not seen for years. The last I knew of him, he was living only a few blocks from where I was staying.

I returned to my room, found his phone number and called him. He was about to leave but urged me to come by for a visit. As he gave the directions, I remembered that he had invited Rachel and me to stay in the house when we vacationed at the beach thirty-five years ago. It was a homey cottage overlooking a lagoon which wound its way into the Gulf through a narrow inlet.

For a long while we reminisced about our growing up years, high school football games and the many things that old friends talk about. But the Holy Spirit seemed to be telling me that I should talk to my friend about Jesus.

I shared my testimony, highlighting my salvation experience. I knew he was raised in church and had a godly mother, but when I asked him if he was on the way to heaven, he gave me an unsure answer. Because of his denomination's belief, he felt he wouldn't make it because he was a divorced and remarried man.

We talked for a long time about Christ's death for man's sins, His love, His forgiveness and how He takes us where we are when we come to Him in a spirit of childlike repentance and trust.

As I returned to the motel that night, I felt that I had been where I was supposed to be. Little did I realize that my friend would be responsible, as a member of the class reunion planning committee, for my being asked to give the devotional at our fortieth celebration a year later.

The invitation came in the form of a poem, highlighting our get together forty years after high school. With the invitation was a request for me to give the devotional. Our class had fifty-four members and a majority of them and their spouses attended, some from hundreds of miles away. Although I had not seen several of my classmates since graduation, I was able to remember the names of most of them.

I had prayed that God would bless me in the devotional so I would give something that would be both inspirational for the group and fit the occasion. My answer came through the invitation. Following are some of my comments:

"When I received the invitation reminding us that it had been forty years since graduation, along with the request to bring the devotional, I thought of the significance of the number forty. Forty is a special number in the Bible.

"God destroyed the earth with a flood that lasted forty days. Jesus was tempted by Satan in the wilderness for forty days. One of the great Bible characters, Moses, had his life divided into three forty-year periods. He was forty years old when he killed the Egyptian who was abusing his fellow Hebrew, a deed which forced him into exile. He had been in exile forty years when God spoke to him at the burning bush and called him to lead his people out of slavery. Although it didn't take long to get the people out of Egypt, it took them forty years of wandering in the wilderness before they got enough faith to possess the land God had promised.

"I hope all of you have already found the faith to accept Christ. As some of you know, I didn't go to church much when I was growing up. But I found Christ forty years ago, during this very part of the summer, while in the Merchant Marines.

"There is going to be another great reunion, and that's the one that will really count. I hope all of us will be there. Please join me as we pray."

I felt the spirit of the Lord as I gave that brief devotional and rejoiced when one of the spouses told me that my remarks were right on target.

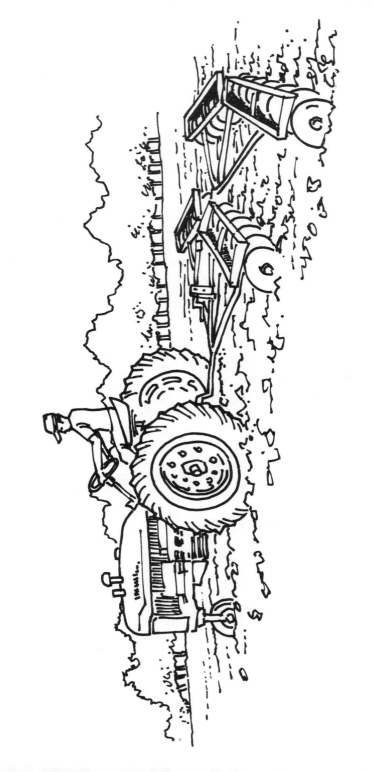

47

This Old Disk is Special

"Daddy, all you have is a piece of junk. This old disk will never be worth anything," said Steve as he made another effort to get a pin back in place that held one of the disk gangs together.

The day was half gone and we had spent most of it trying to fix the old disk so we could prepare the land for planting winter grain in our wildlife plots for the deer and turkey. One after another we had replaced rusty bolts and pins, but we would no sooner get started again when something else would break. Now it was a main pin that kept slipping out of place.

"It's more than a disk; it's special," I explained to Steve as I began to share with him the story of the disk.

I had found the drag type disk at a farm implement shop in Monroe County when I stopped there for a tractor part. It hadn't been used in a long time, but the disk blades were still in good shape. I asked the dealer about the price, thinking it would be what we needed to fix our plots at the farm in Perry County where we had an old International tractor which could only use drag equipment.

The dealer looked at his book and said, "It's a hundred and twenty-five dollars."

I thought the price was high, so I said I would contact him later if I decided to buy it. Too, I thought it would be wider than my pickup so I would need a trailer to haul it. But I kept thinking about the disk and stopped at the shop again about two weeks later when I was returning from a trip.

"I'll give you seventy-five dollars for that piece of junk and take it off your yard so it won't make all your new equipment look bad," I said as I bargained with the dealer about the disk.

He paused, but not for long, and then said, "OK, but you will have to pay the tax." I thought I detected a smile on his face as I agreed, knowing I would have had to pay the tax anyway.

A few days later I drove the fifty miles to Monroeville and they soon had the disk separated into two sections and loaded on my truck. As I passed a ready-mix cement plant on the way home, I had a sudden urge to stop. It hadn't been my intention, but there was the unmistakable feeling that now was the time to find out if I could get a load of ready-mix cement to fix the emergency spillway that carries flood water from the small pond across the roadway at home.

The man in charge of booking the cement and dispatching the trucks said I lived too far from the plant to get cement deliveries in the summer. "It will harden in the truck before we could get there," he said.

Then I shared with Steve how I was about to leave the cement plant when there was the unmistakable urge of the Holy Spirit to witness to the man. "Before I go, may I share something that happened to me several years ago on July 1, 1974?" I asked. When he consented, I told him about the heart attack I had, how I had felt my spirit leave my body and then had heard the music of heaven.

"It's amazing that you should come in here and talk to me about heart trouble after I had another spell with mine just last night," he said. He explained that he had almost died about a year ago when the beat of his heart ran away one night. His wife had gotten him to the doctor who stabilized him with medication, but he occasionally had some problems—including last night.

"Where would you have gone if you had died during one of those spells?" I asked.

Without hesitation he replied, "I guess I would have gone to hell."

"Would you like for me to show you how you can change that destination?"

"I sure would. I want to go to heaven when I die," was his sincere reply.

His name was Willie Earl and he listened very intently as I took my New Testament from my back pocket and began to read the Scriptures of God's love for him as told in John 3:16. I substituted Willie's name for the "world," Jesus' name for God's Son and Willie's name for "whosoever." I explained that "perish" meant "go to hell," but he would never go there if he believed in Jesus and trusted Him for his Savior because He promises eternal life.

Several times we were interrupted by radio calls from truck drivers or drivers bringing their delivery tickets to the office. After each interruption, Willie again gave his hungry attention as the Lord was speaking to his heart. I intermingled my own salvation experience as we traveled the Roman road to the understanding of salvation. "I was on a merchant ship, caught in a hurricane in the Atlantic Ocean, when I got serious with the Lord," I told Willie. "The coal we were carrying had caught fire and we thought we were about to sink. I knew Christ had died for my sins and I also knew I was a sinner and needed to ask Him to forgive my sins if I wanted to go to heaven.

When the Bosun told us we might not be able to stay afloat much longer, I suddenly realized that I would be forever separated from God in my present condition. Like you, I wanted to go to heaven if I died. Right there on the ship, I asked Jesus to save me. The Bible says in Romans 10:13, "Whosoever shall call upon the name of the Lord shall be saved." Just as He saved me on the ship, He will save you right now if you sincerely believe in Him and make repentance for your sins. Would you like to ask Jesus to save you?" I asked.

Willie wanted Jesus. The radio was silent and no one came into the office as he invited Christ into his heart. I didn't have a tract to leave Willie, but promised him something the next time I came to Monroeville. About a month later I brought some printed materials and left them in the dispatch office after being told Willie had gone to lunch. We met at the gate as I was leaving. A big smile was on his face as he recognized me. For a few minutes, he shared his new-found joy. It was a good reunion which will only be better when we get to heaven.

"So that's why the disk is special," I said to Steve as I concluded the story. "If I hadn't bought the disk, I wouldn't have been in Monroeville to tell Willie Earl about Christ." Steve agreed that the disk was special.

The next week I returned to the farm with a hack saw and several new bolts. I replaced the pin that had been slipping and cut away the loose rusty bolts that couldn't be tightened and installed new ones. The disk has worked fine ever since. It is indeed a "special disk."

48

Do We Really Need to Know

I was going through a spiritual dry period in the late summer of 1991. My depressed feeling was brought on because of a witnessing conference I had led at Shocco Springs a couple of months earlier for pastors, deacons and their wives. I had led the witnessing conferences for several years at this annual retreat, but I wanted this one to be something different and special. After much thought, prayer and discussion with Dr. Henry Lyons III, the retreat coordinator, I had asked lay people to help lead a mini Lay-Led Revival with the hopes that the results would be more invitations from churches for Lay Revivals. Lay Revivals usually help church members become more involved in one-on-one witnessing as they observe experienced lay persons witnessing during daily visits while the Revivals are in progress.

Dr. Dale Kennedy, who wrote *Evangelism Explosion*, found through his witnessing experience that, "Witnessing is caught, more than it is taught."

Many church members have discovered their witnessing gift by observing lay men and women witness while they are led by the Holy Spirit during Lay-Led Revivals.

But only a small percentage of the approximately 500 people in attendance at Shocco Springs for the two-day retreat attended our two sessions. I had really worked hard to make the conferences a success. Fred Pinkard, a long-time lay leader from Cleveland, Tennessee, and Barry Barrett, an American Airlines pilot and revival coordinator from Nashville, plus several of our Alabama team members came to help. At the conclusion of the conference, Harold Swearingen, our Alabama coordinator, reported that only a couple of people had expressed any desire to have a revival. Needless to say, I was discouraged about the results.

The weekly jail ministry conducted by Peyton Burford, Jimmy Simpkins and myself was continuing as usual. God always gives me a lift as I feel His presence during our visits. I was sharing Jesus with other people the Lord was putting in front of me each week, plus teaching my Sunday school class. But in spite of all this, I didn't feel uplifted as I brooded over what seemed to be a failure at the conference.

One day, in this somewhat low spirit, I walked around the lake to my special spot by a pine tree and asked God to let me know if my witnessing was getting any results. A few days later, a letter written December 2, 1991, arrived in the mail:

Dear Mr. & Mrs. Dyess,

I just wanted to take this opportunity to thank
you on how Jesus has touched my life through
your ministry.
Grace and peace to you from God our Father
and from the Lord Jesus Christ. Eph. 1:2

Love,

A friend in Christ

In the envelope was a twenty-dollar bill, a ten-
dollar bill and two five-dollar bills. Neither Rachel
or I know whom God might have used to send the
letter. Somehow, I feel that the person who did,
made a sacrificial gift in sending the money. Both
of us have felt very humbled by the letter.

The letter has made us realize that someone
appreciates our witnessing effort. But it has also
made me realize my imperfection of having a
fleshly desire to see things happen that can only be
done by Jesus and not by any of us. The writer had
it right, "Jesus has touched my life." Nothing good
is going to happen in any circumstance unless the
Lord does it. We should be His witness as we go
and leave the results to Him. I'm going to try to do
that from here on out.

One of the inmates at the jail had requested a
big print Bible. Rachel and I agreed that we would
use the money for the Lord's work, so I took part
of it and bought the inmate the Bible which I
presented as a Christmas gift from the friend. We
will use the remainder as the Lord leads.

The above part of this chapter was written several days ago. Its now Monday night, January 13, 1992. I have just returned from the jail. Richard Prichett, the man who got the Bible has a great voice and he led in singing two songs of praise before the Holy Spirit led us in a touching devotional. As I read again what I had written, the Lord gave me the meaning of the letter which I hadn't seen before.

Although God probably used some human being to write the letter, I now believe the verse that was quoted is a direct answer of my prayer from the Lord. "Grace and peace to you from God our Father and the Lord Jesus Christ" (Eph. 1:2 NIV).

49

The Magic Cards

"How did you do that?" was the loud question of the Wilcox County jail inmate as he looked at me through the bars.

"Like I said, these are magic cards," I answered as I turned to the next inmate and began the numbers game with him.

Again, "How did you do that?" vibrated through the cell block as I told his number.

Of the fifteen or so men in the cell block, usually about half would come to the dining area for our weekly witnessing and Bible study service. As I continued the game, I realized every prisoner was crowding into the room, attracted by the "magic cards."

Fred Pinkard had passed out the numbered cards at the witnessing conference described in the previous chapter. That night at the jail, I decided to put a new twist in the game and call them "magic cards." The idea worked. The term "magic" caught the attention of every man in the cell block.

I started my presentation, saying to those present, "Tonight I have some magic cards I want to show you. You can select any number from one to twenty-five and the cards will tell me the number you are thinking." As the first inmate identified the cards that had his number, I put them in my shirt pocket, saying, "Speak to me, cards, and tell me the man's number." After he had seen all the cards, I simply added the numbers which appeared in the top left corner of those he identified, and announced his number.

One by one I played the game with each prisoner who came forward. "I plan to have copies of the cards printed. I'll give each of you a set and show you how you can be a magician," I said while explaining that there is no such thing as magic, but that somebody had arranged the numbers so that we always got the right answer.

There were some hard fellows in the cell, but through the cards I had their attention. "We just played a game, now I want to show you something real. On the back of card one is a question. Let me read it to you. 'Do you know for certain you have eternal life?' If you don't know the answer to that question, let's read what the Bible says about how we can find the way to heaven."

The Holy Spirit was powerful that night as I read the Scripture verses on the back of the cards telling how they could be saved. When I gave an invitation, nine of the men came forward and asked Jesus to save them. I went to another cell block and saw the same kind of results. I knew that night that the cards were a useful tool in sharing Jesus.

A printer gave me a price to print a thousand sets of the cards. I played the game with him and began to explain what I wanted on the back of each card. "On the back of card one, print this question: 'Do you know for certain you have eternal life?'"

I was about to add, "The Bible says...," when he interrupted me to blurt out, "No, I don't know if I have eternal life."

"Would you like to know?" I asked.

"Yes, I want to know," he answered.

As we read the cards and talked about how we can know Jesus, again I saw the power of the Holy Spirit speak through the Scripture verses, and I lead that printer to know Christ. I saw that same power repeated many times during the next year as the Lord put people in front of me to receive the 1,000 sets of cards. One man who came to the farm to buy pecans, asked Jesus to save him in my yard; another in our Christmas tree orchard. I always tried to share with each customer. Store clerks, waitresses, service station employees and business acquaintances all were willing to play the magic card game and then receive God's plan for eternal life.

"Let me show you my magic cards," became my opener. "You do believe in magic? If you will think of a number between one and twenty-five, I'll let the cards tell me the number. Or I'll let them tell me your age." (Sixty-three is the top number on the cards).

People relax during the numbers game and are not defensive when I show them how the system works and then say, "That's a game we just played;

there is no such thing as magic. But let me show you something that is not a game, something real. Read the first sentence on the back of card one. That's a real question we all must answer." If the prospect hesitates, I usually say, "It's not important what you tell me. You know, and God knows, what your answer is. If you do know you're on your way to heaven, read the cards as they are numbered and share them with someone who doesn't know. If you are not sure about your own answer, read the cards and do what the Bible says we must each do, in order to have eternal life."

It doesn't take long to play the game and share the cards. For example, I was in Montgomery, Alabama, during the Christmas rush at a Sam's Discount store. I hadn't been in the store for a while and I had to renew my membership card. When I reached the head of the line, a tired looking young man made my picture, took the necessary information and issued me a new card.

"Would you like to see my magic cards?" I said, explaining that it would only take a minute. His tired expression brightened as we quickly played the numbers game.

"That's interesting," he said as I revealed his number and explained how the system worked.

"The important part is on the back," I said as I showed him the eternal life question.

Slowly he shook his head, "No, I don't know if I have eternal life."

"If you will read each card as they are numbered, they will tell you how you can know," I said as I turned to leave.

Before I could go, he stopped me with these words. "Mister, I thank you for taking the time to talk to me." I believe God had already prepared this man's heart to receive Christ and he was just waiting for someone to tell him how. The whole episode hadn't taken more than two minutes.

Giving away the cards is another example of leaving the results to the Lord. We probably won't know many of the results on this earth. Our job is to share the plan of salvation so everyone will know what the Lord would have each person do to be saved. The Philippian jailer didn't know how. Paul and Silas told him and he was saved. As Christians, that's our calling.

```
 1  3  5  7  9 11 13 15
17 19 21 23 25 27 29 31
33 35 37 39 41 43 45 47
49 51 53 55 57 59 61 63
```

1

Do you know for certain that you have eternal life?

The Bible says:

"For God so loved the world that He gave His only begotten Son that whosoever believeth in Him should not perish, but have **Everlasting Life**." (John 3:16)

Jesus died on the cross for your sins.

```
 2  3  6  7 10 11 14 15
18 19 22 23 26 27 30 31
34 35 38 39 42 43 46 47
50 51 54 55 58 59 62 63
```

2

The Bible says:

"For all have sinned and fallen short of the glory of God". (Romans 3:23)

"For the wages of sin is death; but the gift of God is **Eternal Life** through Jesus Christ our Lord." (Romans 6:23)

```
 4  5  6  7 12 13 14 15
20 21 22 23 28 29 30 31
36 37 38 39 44 45 46 47
52 53 54 55 60 61 62 63
```

3

We are saved by grace (the goodness of God) through faith; not of yourselves: it is the gift of God. Not of works, lest any man should boast. (Ephesians 2:8,9)

The Bible says that the spirit which brings salvation appears to all men. (Titus 2:11)

Jesus says in Revelations 3:20: Behold, I stand at the door and knock; If any man hear my voice, and open the door, I will come in to him, and will sup with him and he with me.

```
 8  9 10 11 12 13 14 15
24 25 26 27 28 29 30 31
40 41 42 43 44 45 46 47
56 57 58 59 60 61 62 63
```

4

How do we invite Jesus into our hearts?

If we will confess with our mouth the Lord Jesus, and believe in our heart that God raised Him from the dead, we can be saved. For with the heart man believes unto righteousness; and with the mouth confession is made unto salvation. (Romans 10:9,10)

```
16 17 18 19 20 21 22 23
24 25 26 27 28 29 30 31
48 49 50 51 52 53 54 55
56 57 58 59 60 61 62 63
```

5

The Bible says:

"Whosoever shall call upon the name of the Lord shall be saved." (Romans 10:13)

Call upon the Lord to save you by praying this prayer:

Lord Jesus, I need You. Thank You for dying on the cross for my sins.

6

I know I have sinned and need Your forgiveness. I ask You to come into my life, forgive my sins, and be my Lord and Savior. Thank You for saving me and giving me **Eternal Life**. Lord, help me daily to live for You.

```
32 33 34 35 36 37 38 39
40 41 42 43 44 45 46 47
48 49 50 51 52 53 54 55
56 57 58 59 60 61 62 63
```

If I can help you, please call
Ernest Dyess
Rt. 2, Box 263
Camden, AL 36726
205-682-4623

260

50

George Strong—My Unforgettable Scoutmaster

It was noon and still there wasn't a cloud in the sky. I had to make a decision. Should I attend the Fiftieth Anniversary ceremony of Camden Boy Scout Troop 94 and observe two young men from my church fellowship, Gaines Jonakin and Neil Wilder, be inducted into the Eagle Court of Honor; or should I spray my two-acre muscadine vineyard?

Normally it wouldn't have been a big deal to spray the vineyard, but the fruit would soon be ripe and the excessive rains were ideal for breeding a fungus, causing "ripe rot." The expensive spray had to have at least twenty-four hours of dry weather to be effective, and this was the first dry day in over a week.

As I labored in the hot July sun to get the sprayer serviced, I thought of my own Boy Scout days in Rosinton, Alabama, some fifty years earlier. My Scoutmaster was George Strong who had come to the rural Baldwin County community as principal of the school which had eight grades and three teachers other than himself. Mr. Strong loved sports and he loved children.

Years later, I began to realize all the things Mr. Strong did for our youth, including using his own very limited financial resources during the Depression of the late thirties and the early forties. Somehow he managed to build a workshop outside the school so we could learn basic woodworking skills. We didn't have a gym for basketball, so he built an outdoor court. He would pack us in his car and drive to most of the schools in the county to play games, and we won our share.

In the classroom he excelled, bringing out the best of our abilities as he rotated discussion time between the seventh and eighth grade. Self-images are made or broken by people we trust. I remember a day George Strong raised my self-image by helping me realize that I was as capable as my classmates. He had assigned us to write a geography paper on a number of foreign countries we were studying. After the papers were graded, he read aloud to the class the paper he considered to be the best. "I gave this one an 'A,'" he told the class without giving the name of the student. The other children learned it was my paper. They probably knew it by just looking at the skinny kid who was beaming with pride.

In the Boy Scout program Mr. Strong instilled moral values that last a lifetime. If I ever knew, I can't remember how he became interested in scouting. It sure wasn't reasonable that one man could form a troop in a rural community that had only one store and no means of financial support, especially in the midst of a great depression. Somehow he did it. Many of us couldn't afford a uniform, but he made everything else available for becoming a good Boy Scout—from manuals to pup tents for regular camping expeditions. Each summer we camped for a week on nearby Styx River, where he kept us busy with day games and night games while teaching survival cooking methods and a host of scouting skills.

Under Mr. Strong's leadership, the older scouts erected a log hut on the bank of an abandoned mill pond, where we were able to progress through the scout ranks. Our troop usually won many of the honors at county "Jamborees" because of the dedicated training of our Scoutmaster.

Mr. Strong didn't overlook the spiritual part of scouting, making sure that we all participated regularly in scout services at a local church.

World War II brought new activities for our troop, gathering old newspapers and other salvageable recycling materials for the war effort. Mr. Strong was past the age of military service, but I think school officials decided his talents were needed in a larger school. When he left Rosinton, Mrs. Kennedy, the fifth and sixth grade teacher, became the principal. No one volunteered to be Scoutmaster, so our troop died. But the values Mr. Strong taught us lived on.

As the years passed, I began to recognize some of the contributions my Scoutmaster made to my life. Every time I tie a square knot, or two half-hitches, I remember my "Tenderfoot" efforts at knot tying on my way to becoming a "2nd Class Scout." When I was in the army, compass and map reading were "old hat" to me because we learned those skills, plus a lot of others, in Boy Scouts.

Maturity also brought another memory of the character of Mr. Strong. My classmates and I were talking about a community dove hunt. I commented that I couldn't go on the hunt because I didn't have a gun. Mr. Strong, who was listening to our conversation, said, "I have a double-barreled shotgun I'll sell you. I don't hunt much, so if you want it, I'll let you have it for four dollars."

My only income was about a dollar a week from my Grit paper route, but I knew I could handle four dollars. I was a joyful young man when he brought the gun to me the next day. Years later, I realized Mr. Strong didn't sell me the gun for four dollars, he gave me the gun for four dollars.

I never went back to live in Baldwin County after finishing high school at Robertsdale, but I often thought of looking for Mr. Strong and thanking him personally for his contribution to my life. I never did, and it is one of the big regrets I have today.

But this Saturday afternoon, as I did the last service work on the sprayer in preparation for spraying the vineyard, I made a commitment to attend the recognition ceremony of Troop 94. I said a silent prayer: "Lord, I want to dedicate this afternoon in honor of my old Scoutmaster, Mr. George Strong."

I hadn't recited the Scout oath in years, but phrase after phrase returned to my memory as I drove to town:

"On my honor I will do my best To do my duty to God and my country and to obey the Scout Law; To help other people at all times; To keep myself physically strong, mentally awake, and morally straight."

I arrived at the scout grounds a little early. Already the place was bustling with people. Jonakin and Wilder would become the fifty-sixth and fifty-seventh Eagle Scouts to emerge from the troop in its fifty years of existence. A majority of the Eagles, with their families, were present for the anniversary, some traveling hundreds of miles for the special day. Before the program started, I had the opportunity to talk briefly with Max Baggett, the present Scoutmaster, and I shared with him a few thoughts of my scout days and what Mr. Strong meant to me.

"Why don't you make a few comments about your scouting experiences?" Max asked. I accepted, with the understanding he would not call upon me if the program was too long. An out-of-town guest speaker and some of the Eagle Scouts presented an exciting program as they highlighted Christian values and the merits of Scouting. Any additional comments would have been out of order.

If there had been time, I would have spoken of Mr. Strong's dedication as a Scoutmaster; my failure to go back and thank him for what he did for me; and then I would have shared a story about a foreign missionary who had completed his last assignment.

The missionary had become an old man after many terms overseas and was coming back to the

United States to retire. When his plane touched down at an American city, a well-known politician got aboard, and then the plane continued the flight to both men's destination. When they arrived, a brass band and many people were there to welcome the politician home. The old missionary remained in his seat while the politician was basking in the limelight. But missionaries are flesh and blood. They too have fleshly feelings the same as you and I, so he said a prayer. It went something like this: "Lord, you know I have given my life to you. This politician has all these people to meet him when he gets home; but I don't have a single person to meet me after all my years of service."

When the missionary completed his prayer, a still small voice said to him, "But you're not home yet!"

Mr. Strong is home now. The best I could do was thank his son for what his daddy did for me on this earth. When I get to heaven, I am going to look up Mr. Strong and thank him personally.

If I had spoken, I would have also told the Scout leaders to always remember in their moments of discouragement, "You, too, are not home yet." At that heavenly homecoming you will be recognized for your long hours and unselfish dedication in shaping the countless lives of our youth.

51

It's Malignant

As I lay on the mobile bed in a lobby leading to the operating room, I thought about the heart attack I had eighteen years before. I remembered hearing the heavenly music and feeling my spirit leave my body while I drifted into unconsciousness on the seat of the car. Would my heart stand this operation? Would I hear the music again? Would this be my time to make the total journey to heaven?

Across the way a doctor worked with another patient. He glanced at me for a moment as I meditated about my assurance of being with the Lord if He called.

This prostate cancer operation which I was about to have had brought me in contact with a host of people and given me many opportunities to share Jesus. It wasn't what I wanted to hear when a doctor in another city said, "It's malignant." Nevertheless, as the reality of his diagnosis sank in, I was able to tell him about my heart attack, the music I had heard and my assurance of life after this life. His interruption, and comments of explanation of my near-death experience to his internee, made me know he needed to hear about Jesus. "No, Doctor, you may believe whatever you wish, but I know there is going to be 'life after life'. I know it's late, but since I'm the last patient, please give me a minute to explain how I know."

He nodded in agreement as I took out a set of the magic cards, showed him the numbers game, but more importantly, the question, "Do you know if you have eternal life?" I briefly shared what Christ had done for all mankind, and showed him the verses of Scripture on the back of the cards that would lead to his knowing about eternal life if he would believe. Without comment, he put the cards in his pocket as we said good-by. The results? I don't know. It's not my business to know. The Lord has commissioned all Christians to "Go and tell the things we have seen and heard." The drawing, the convicting, the visiting by the Spirit for salvation, will be done by the Lord. But there was one result I did know. The next day, the internee went out of his way to speak to me in the lobby. I think he believes in a resurrected Jesus.

Dr. Caldwell DeBardeleben, my heart doctor who had discovered my problem through a routine examination, made arrangements for me to see Dr. Joe Davis for treatment in Montgomery. Dr. Davis recommended surgery rather than radiation. During the month prior to the scheduled surgery, I was to give four units of blood at the Montgomery Red Cross Center. The donors' room had six couches arranged in a circle, which allowed every one to see each other and talk as we gave blood. It was the perfect place to have fun with the numbers game. Sometimes I told people their age, sometimes I told the number they were thinking.

As I gave each person a set of cards and explained how the game worked, I referred to the question on the back of card one, "Do you know for certain you have eternal life?" Usually, I didn't wait for an answer, but said, "It's not important what you tell me. What really counts is between you and the Lord. If you already know the right answer, share the cards with someone who doesn't. If you are unsure about your relationship with Christ, read the back of the cards which explain what the Bible says about finding the way to heaven."

As a military man gave blood, I saw the intense interest in his eyes. I was led to share the story of how the Lord saved me and other parts of my personal testimony. I could see the Holy Spirit speaking to this man. As I walked out the door, he returned my wave of good-by from his couch.

Another day, I shared the cards with a man in the lobby as we both waited to give the blood. "I work with the youth in my church. I am going to get cards printed for my witnessing," he said as we shared what God was doing in our lives.

A young man who worked for the Red Cross walked into the waiting lobby and struck up a conversation with a co-worker. "I have visited several churches, and I am going to visit several more. When I find the right one, I'll join," he said as they discussed church denominations.

"If you will sit by me for a minute I'll show you how you can find the right answer," I said.

It didn't take long to explain to him that it wasn't the church that saved people, just Jesus. "When we trust Jesus, he will guide us to the right church for worship, fellowship and place of service," I said as we discussed what the Bible says a man must do in order to be saved.

But the experience I remember most began the first week I gave blood. I had shared with everyone in the donor room except a working nurse. She was the happy-go-lucky type who talked a lot but didn't seem to stay in one place long enough for me to bring her into a conversation. I didn't think so, but she was listening as I shared the cards with the others. My blood was being packed away and I was about to go when she said, "You didn't tell me my age." Rachel had warned me that I had better be careful about telling the age of ladies if they were past thirty. This nurse, I'll call her Ann, was past thirty.

"Are you sure you want me to tell your age? I could let you select a number and I'll tell you the number."

"No, tell me my age," she said, as if believing I couldn't do it.

"You lack one year being half way to a special number," I replied as I indicated to her that she was 49. Without reply she walked away before I could say more. But the following week, it was Ann who took me into a small office to do the paperwork before drawing blood. As she repeated all the questions about my life history, I said, "Last week you didn't wait for me to give you a set of the cards so you can be a magician, too."

"You were going to give me the cards?"

"I sure was. Let me show you how they work. More importantly, let me show you a question on the back of card one. 'Do you know for sure you have eternal life?'"

Ann looked at me for a long moment, then very emphatically said, "Yes, I know." With that response she began to tell me one of the most heartbreaking stories I have ever heard.

She told about growing up in another state in a fairly large family. "I have a brother who is close to my age. We were as close as a brother and sister can be. After high school, he went to seminary and I went to nursing school. During his last year at the seminary, he came home and told me he was dropping out. 'I can't be a preacher. I no longer believe there is a God. One of my professors told me I could still be a good preacher even if I didn't believe in God. I don't think I can, so I am dropping out of school.' That night, I fell on my knees and begged God to help my brother. That's been several years ago, but I have been asking Him ever since. Last week my brother called, and he's coming to see me. He wants to talk to me about the Lord. I've always been considered the black sheep of the family. What am I going to tell him?" she asked with tear-stained eyes.

"God will lead and give you the right words," I said as the nurse who was to take my blood beckoned.

Back home, I couldn't get Ann and her brother out of my mind. Needless to say, I have prayed for them many times. I thought about my own questions of God's reality as a youth and how I had prayed for God to show me if He was real. I made a copy of chapter one of this book to give to Ann the next week. I thought about my atheist college professor, who finally said yes to God after He had revealed His reality to him. I made copies of that chapter, plus the one about the heavenly music, for Ann's brother.

Ann wasn't at the center the next week, but another nurse gave the envelope to her when she came off the bloodmobile that night. She was in the field again the last time I went to the center, so I don't know the results of Ann's visit with her brother; but I do know that God is sensitive to our prayers, especially when we become concerned for others. I believe God will answer Ann's prayers and reveal himself in a special way to her brother.

Intermingled with the Red Cross visits were trips to the Montgomery Radiology clinic and a cardiology center. Each of these visits gave me several opportunities to share Jesus and pass out the card tracts. As I shared with a beautiful, Christian young lady in Dr. Porters office while waiting for a treadmill test, her comment about Christian witnessing, or maybe I should say, the lack of it, really struck home. If I remember correctly, she had worked there for over five years and encountered a steady stream of heart patients. "You are the first person who has ever wanted to talk about Jesus since I have been here," she said as we discussed how we ought to be sharing the most important good news of mankind to a lost and dying world.

As I continued to wait in the operating lobby, I thought about the doctor I was trusting to perform my surgery. He had classified me as a B1, which means, although not the best, the odds were in my favor for a successful operation. During my evaluation visit, he had explained how patients were classified A1, A2; B1, B2; C1, C2; and D1, D2. He pointed out that other conditions, such as the degree of the cancer's progress, could change the classification to a D2, the worst stage. I had commented, "If you become a D2, I suppose that's terminal?"

"No, it doesn't mean it's terminal. Over four years ago I operated on a man who was a D2, and he is alive and going about his business today. A person is not terminal until they die," said Dr. Joe Davis very emphatically. Later I would hear Dr. Davis say, "Only God determines when a person dies." I knew I had the right doctor.

Suddenly, as if out of nowhere, Dr. Davis was standing by my side in the operating room lobby, "Are you ready, Mr. Dyess?"

People talk about peace in many ways. Christians talk about the peace that only God can give when we face crisis and the possibility of passing into eternity with our Lord. Throughout this whole ordeal, God had given His peace to me as He heard the prayers of my many Christian friends, including inmates in the county jail, who had faithfully prayed in my behalf. It was easy to reply to the doctor, "I'm ready."

"Let's have prayer together before we go," was his response.

He asked me to lead and I committed myself and Doctor Davis to the Lord's care and thanked Him for His goodness to us. The anesthetist came and before I realized it, life stood still for me.

Suddenly there was a dim light, and then it grew brighter. Was I in heaven? In the distance I could hear my name being called. Again I heard my name, but it wasn't the Lord. It was a woman's voice. Maybe it's an angel, I thought. She was pretty enough to be an angel with her golden hair and sweet face. "Are you cold, Mr. Dyess?" were her words, which brought me to the realization that I wasn't in heaven, but rather a hospital recovery room, as I saw a drainage tube protruding from my body.

"You're cold and we're going to warm you with another blanket," she said as she tucked it in around me.

I was still very sleepy and I wanted to close my eyes and forget about the difficulty of talking, but her questions wouldn't let me do that. "How do you feel now?" required an answer.

My voice was weak and I had trouble making the sounds, but she seemed to understand every word. As we talked, I remembered my commitment before coming to the hospital, to share Jesus with every person He put in front of me. I had tried to share with a man shortly after we arrived on Tuesday morning. I didn't get very far before he let me know he wasn't interested. The sweet aroma of the large basket of freshly picked muscadines

Rachel and I had brought from our vineyard filled the admittance lobby as I returned to my seat beside Rachel. I said a silent prayer: "Lord, I can't do anything unless you prepare the way. You're the vine and I am a branch. Just as these muscadines would not have grown without nourishment from the vine, neither can I be an effective witness unless you are with me. Lord, I want to be your man, if you want me."

I was barely seated when a teen-aged boy and his mother took a seat near us. The boy had a long fiber cast reaching from a foot to an armpit. "Do you have a football injury?" I asked. He replied that he did and said he had already had surgery. He had the physical characteristics of a running back. When he affirmed his position, I asked, "Are you a good football player?"

As I looked into his face, I sensed that his answer was not one of conceit, just fact. "Yeah, I'm pretty good."

"I'll bet you are good. While we're waiting, play a game with me," I said as I showed him a set of the cards. "I'll let these cards tell me how old you are," as I showed him the numbers and declared that he was 15.

"I'm giving you this set of cards, and you can take them to school with you and have fun with your friends," I said as I showed him how the system always gave the right answer. "That's a game we just played. Now let me show you something about the real game of life. Read that first sentence on the back of card one. If you don't know about eternal life yet, take the cards home with you and read how the Bible declares you can know. From what you already told me, I can see that you want to be a great football player. That's a fine goal. If you work hard, the Lord may very well bless you to be a good player. Sometimes players do get hurt, and they can't do what they want; but if you trust Jesus to guide your life, He will direct you into a new pathway better than the one you were traveling. If something like that happens, you will be able to look back and see that the Lord knew what was best for you all along."

By this time the boy's mother was involved in our conversation. She told me she was a Christian and she wanted the best for her son. We talked about role models that football players could be for their peers. We discussed how everyone looked up to football players, and how they could lead in the right way as well as the wrong way. As the admittance secretary called my name, I could see in the eyes of the Cloverdale Junior High School running back that he wanted to be a good role model.

God heard the prayer I prayed about being his witness and prepared every one else He put in front of me to listen, as I shared His plan of eternal salvation. After we checked into the room, word spread quickly that we had the muscadine basket. As we shared the muscadines, we shared the cards and Jesus with many people who came throughout the day.

Now in the recovery room, I thought for a brief moment about the cards. If I had a set, I could share them with the nurse; however, I knew I didn't need cards to tell someone about the things Christ had done for me. The cards were just an easy way to start. I don't remember how the Lord began our spiritual conversation, but for the next hour we talked about how God was real in our lives. We talked about witnessing, and how we can be a witness 'as we go' in our daily lives. She said she was presently enrolled in a witnessing class in her church. We talked about the power of our personal testimony as being the greatest witnessing tool of all. We agreed that lost people will believe a lay person, when we share from our hearts the things we have seen and heard.

Even though my speech was slow, I could feel the power of the Holy Spirit as we shared. Maybe the recovery room time was a glimpse of what heaven will be like, when we will have an eternity to share those very special moments which God gives His children.

After my body temperature warmed, I was taken to ICU where I would experience the most difficult night of my hospital stay. Somehow I was different from most patients, because the epidural relief procedure did not stop the pain which became more and more intense. Two shots of morphine didn't help much. Finally at 3:30 A.M., another drug gave relief and I eased into a restful sleep. But the hours preceding the relief were made easier by a sweet nurse who did her best to ease my pain. She encouraged my conversation as she told of the muscadines she enjoyed during her teenage visits to her grandfather's farm near Wedowee. As the pain grew worse, God made it easier for me to bear by opening the door for me to share my personal testimony. When we have someone to listen as we talk about Jesus, the pain is always easier. I believe Paul and Silas realized that as they witnessed to their fellow Phillipian prisoners, although they were hurting after being beaten with many stripes.

I was assigned a room after a day in ICU. One by one, I played the numbers game with the staff of each shift, as they checked my vital signs and looked after my every need. No one left without having to ponder the question of their relationship with Christ. Each person carried with them the scriptural references that can lead to eternal life. Sometimes my eyes were heavy with sleep when nurses came in the late night hours, but I always shared because I was afraid the shift might change before I saw the person again. I wasn't always the one who began the witnessing conversation. One night a beautiful nurse came to my room. As I was trying to awaken, she noticed my Bible beside the bed. "Are you a Christian?" she asked.

"I was about to share with you; but I believe you already know the same Jesus I know," I answered. The floor was quiet and for the next thirty minutes she sat beside my bed as we talked about the Christian life.

She was concerned abut her husband. "I want to grow spiritually and he doesn't seem to be as interested as I am. But he has begun to read his Bible. We work different shifts, and the other day I came home and found him reading for the first time. Our daughter told me later that he had been reading it for a long time."

As we talked on that night and again the next day, I discovered she had high ideals for her husband. She wanted him to be a spiritual leader, not only in her home, but also in her church. It also crept into our conversation that she wanted him to be an ideal husband. "He is not as affectionate toward me as I would like," was one of her comments while adding some of his other weaknesses.

"I want you to do something for me," I said as I prepared to offer her a challenge. "Take a sheet of paper and draw a line down the middle, then list all of the faults of your husband on one side, all his good qualities on the other, and see what you come up with. Try to think of everything. For instance if he doesn't chase other women, write 'faithful husband' on the plus side."

"You have just reminded me of something I was thinking not long ago," she said. "We were close friends with another couple. They seemed perfect together. The husband was always doing little things for his wife that made me wish my husband was like him. Later we learned that all the time he was having an affair with another woman, and now they are divorced. I still have my husband."

"That's the idea; think about every good quality you can. Then do two things more: first, give your husband to the Lord and ask Him to make him what He would have him be, not what you want him to be; secondly, you love him and give yourself to him just the way he is—faults, good qualities and all. Then you can step back and watch God work in his life. If you will do that, I think you will be surprised at how happy your life will be," I said.

She told me a relative was keeping the children, and she and her husband were going away for a long weekend to the mountains. When I left the hospital, she gave me a good-by hug and confided that she could hardly wait until they left that evening.

Another nurse said she had taken her cards home and given them to her little girl, who was learning to read. "Last night she showed them to her grand-mother, and this morning she read the plan of salvation to me as I was driving her to school."

I was down to my final two sets of cards when four nurses came into the room as we were making preparations to go home. I had talked with two of them the day before. I played the game with the two new nurses, asked the question, and passed out the last cards. I sensed this was one of God's special times. As the Spirit led, I shared my testimony in depth with the four ladies. "When we are faced with a time like I have been through this past week, we need to know we have eternal life. We also need to know this when we are not going through a crisis, because we don't have the promise of tomorrow. Jesus has already paid for all our sins on the cross. All we have to do is believe in Him, make Him our Lord, ask forgiveness for our sins and publicly accept Him as our Savior." I knew God was speaking through me. I could tell by looking into the eyes of the ladies.

Witnessing for our Lord is the only thing I know of that assures success before we start. God promises this in the fifty-fifth chapter of Isaiah.

"So shall my word be that goeth forth out of my mouth: it shall not return unto me void, but it shall accomplish that which I please and it shall prosper in the thing whereto I send it. For ye shall go out with joy, and be led forth with peace: the mountains and the hills shall break forth before you into singing, and all the trees of the field shall clap their hands" (Isa. 55:11-12).

My final comment to the group was, "There were times when I hurt while I was here, but for me, it has been a good week."

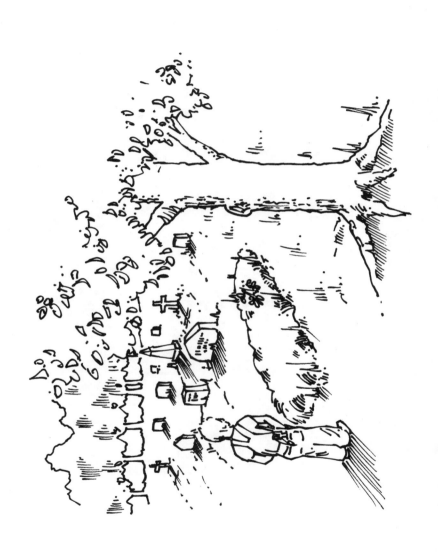

No Headstone Needed

A car horn blew for my attention as I was about to enter the walk leading to the Wilcox Female Institute building. "Would you like to escort a young lady to the meeting while I park the car?" asked the driver, Janet Phillippi.

"It will be my pleasure," I responded as I recognized Mrs. Viola Liddell, a special friend and longtime encourager. It was Mrs. Viola who had inspired me to continue this book after I became discouraged during its early stages. Since she had written two books and numerous short stories and articles, I valued her judgment and caught a new drive through her encouragement and suggestions.

I don't think Mrs. Viola knew I had been asked to give the devotional that day as I assisted her up the walk. I had some apprehension about the subject I had chosen and wasn't sure as to how it would be received. But as we slowly made our way into the historic old building which had been restored as a meeting place by the Wilcox Historical

Society, I could feel Mrs. Viola's positive warmth and I knew every thing would be all right.

A good crowd was present for the Historical Society's monthly meeting as I read one verse of Scripture, Ecclesiastes 1:4: "One generation passeth away, and another generation cometh: but the earth abideth for ever."

I told the gathering how the verse had first caught my attention as the caption of a poster showing a freshly-plowed field some twenty years ealier. I had used the poster to illustrate a talk about our natural resources to a ladies' club in Thomasville while industrially employed. "Man may abuse and alter our God-given resources, but the earth will abide forever," was my comment.

I also said the verse had carried me back to my young years when I was growing up in rural South Alabama. "As a lad, I often visited the country cemeteries. I liked to read the headstone inscriptions and determine the length of life of those buried there. I was intrigued by other information sometimes on the headstones, such as where the person was born, and family relationships. Sometimes the words were "Rest in Peace," or "Gone, But Not Forgotten." Then I began to notice that some graves had no markers. Maybe a wooden board which had rotted away. Sometimes the sunken outline of a grave was the only indication that a person was buried there. This discovery greatly troubled me.

"I began to think about the possibility of my own death. It was during the years of the Great Depression and money was hard to come by in my family. Suppose I died and and was buried without a headstone. I would become like the unknown graves and people might never know that I had ever lived. I never shared this thought, but it was in the back of my mind as I grew into a teenager."

I told of joining the Merchant Marines when I was eighteen and my conversion experience during the storm at sea. "Until I made my decision for Christ, I thought I might perish in the ocean without even an unmarked grave. From that moment when I told the Lord I wanted to be with Him if the ship went under, He began to take away my need for a marker.

"I am not saying that we shouldn't put tombstones on our loved ones' graves, or that history is not important. History is important and I believe we should record the events which happen during our own lifetime. For example, I would like to know more about my family's early days in Baldwin County. I can vaguely remember my great-aunt Sallie who lived to be ninety-three. She was the family historian who told tales of my great-grandfather's move from Monroe County to Rosinton by covered wagon about 1888. I'd like to know more about their struggles to convert a section of fertile timber land to row crops. But I don't think anyone recorded much about those early years. I encourage all of you to write about the highlights of your life. Your thoughts will be precious to your descendants.

"But more important than history is where we will spend eternity. Someday my family will bury this body of mine. But I won't be there. I will already be with the Lord because of what happened on the ship."